THE MILFORD SERIES

Popular Writers of Today

VOLUME THREE

7 6 9 1

The
Farthest Shores
of Ursula K.
Le Guin

George Edgar Slusser

R. REGINALD
THE 𝕭𝖔𝖗𝖌𝖔 𝕻𝖗𝖊𝖘𝖘
SAN BERNARDINO, CALIFORNIA
MCMLXXVI

Library of Congress Cataloguing in Publication Data

Slusser, George Edgar
  The farthest shores of Ursula K. Le Guin.

  (Popular Writers of today; v. 3) (The Milford series)
  1. Le Guin, Ursula K., 1929-   — Criticism and
interpretation.   I. Title.
PS3562.E42.Z9   813'.5'4   76-41929
ISBN 0-89370-205-6

Excerpts from *Rocannon's World*
Copyright Ⓒ 1966 by Ace Books, Inc.
Reprinted by permission of Ace Books.

Excerpts from *Planet of Exile; City of Illusions.*
Copyright Ⓒ 1966, 1967 resp. by Ursula K. Le Guin.
Reprinted by permission of Ace Books.

Excerpts from *The Left Hand of Darkness; The Tombs of
Atuan; The Farthest Shore; The Dispossessed.*
Copyright Ⓒ 1969, 1970/1971, 1972, 1974 resp. by
Ursula K. Le Guin.
Reprinted by permission of Virginia Kidd.

Excerpts from *From Elfland to Poughkeepsie.*
Copyright Ⓒ 1973 by Pendragon Press.
Reprinted by permission of Virginia Kidd.

Excerpts from *The Word for World Is Forest.*
Copyright Ⓒ 1972 by Harlan Ellison.
Reprinted by permission of Virginia Kidd.

R. Reginald, The Borgo Press is a wholly-owned subsidary of
Lynwyck Realty and Investment Company, Inc., P.O. Box
2845, San Bernardino, CA 92406.

First Printing — — — — September, 1976

1 2 3 4 5 6 7 8 9 10

INTRODUCTION

In terms of quality alone, it is difficult to speak of development in the fiction of Ursula K. Le Guin. Her writing has been good from the start. She has published short stories of high quality, selectively, over a period of thirteen years. Since 1966, she has written nine novels. Even the worst of these, *The Lathe of Heaven* is imaginative and ambitious, far superior to most SF being produced today. There is little doubt that Le Guin is one of the best writers currently working in the science fiction and fantasy genres. Apparently at the height of her powers, she promises much.

Nor has her world view changed or altered significantly since the beginning. Some recent critics have spoken of an evolution in Le Guin's ethos — from an early existentialism through a quiet "Taoist" period to strong political activism in the latest works. Such a development is doubtful. She has never embraced either extreme, the fear and trembling of the isolated individual in an absurd universe, or the security of the collective cause. Her best fiction, in fact, examines the possibility of balance between the individual and his world. Le Guin has always believed strongly in such balance, in the dynamics of polarity. Taoism is not an interlude; it is and has always been the strongest single force behind her work, the mold that shapes novel after novel, and binds them one to another in a coherent pattern of human history. Her use of oriental wisdom is highly personal, the creative adaptation of a philosophical system to a literary genre long dominated by a harshly western vision of evolution and technological progress.

A few critics have also linked her vision with the New England Transcendentalists; Le Guin herself has denied it. It is more prudent to say that both share a common source, and that Le Guin's return to it only proves the viability of an old tradition in American letters.

Le Guin's universe obeys less the law of dialectics than that of polarity. In no case is a higher third born of the confrontation of opposites. Le Guin's "way" is not progressive, nor does it view man as working towards some prescribed end in a distant future. Her universe is ongoing, but not open-ended, for the pattern, the equilibrium, is ever-present; the more things change, the more they remain the same. But how free is the individual man to act in such a world? Indeed, does the word "individual" have any meaning here at all? In the final pages of *The Dispossessed* a Hainishman, Ketho, member of the oldest race, puts the matter thus: "We have been civilized for a thousand millennia . . . We have tried everything. Anarchism with the rest. But *I* have not tried it. They say there is nothing new under any sun. But if each life is not new, each single life, then why are we born?" We are born not to mourn the fact that all is fixed, permanent. We are born rather to adapt our individual lives to these patterns, to live and die. Ketho balances each single life against the whole. Individual man is important, for he is the prime mover, the source of power. What counts is the living itself, the means without the ends. In such a universe, man cannot make himself (or it) better, but he can make himself wiser.

To study Le Guin's novels is to study a complex organism that is growing and expanding harmoniously according to a central law of balance. This growth takes two forms. First, there is a shift in focus away from the celebration of balance and toward the problematics of balance, a shift which brings the individual closer to the center of this world, as maker and breaker of equilibrium. From novel to novel, man's relationship to the whole, and the nature and composition of that whole, become increasingly complex. Second, to render this complexity, there are important changes in form. Le Guin's later novels are much more elaborate, more concrete, more realistic. In place of vaguely stylized "worlds," we find carefully drawn societies; instead of "heroes," multifaceted, believable characters. Le Guin rapidly abandons the classic impersonal narrator, so dear to many old pseudo-epics and space operas, and begins to experiment with point of view. First a story is told from the limited perspective of one mind, and then through two or more centers of consciousness; diaries, interpolated tales, elaborate fictions of the editor, all have their place. Simple linear storytelling gives way to flashbacks, skillful juxtapositions of narrated time. Here, on this level, we may speak of synthesis. For what is happening, and will probably continue to happen in Le Guin's fiction, is an interesting merger of genres — the literature of speculation, science fiction and fantasy, with that of personal relationships and manners, the so-called "mainstream" novel.

THE EARLY HAINISH NOVELS

From the start, Le Guin's writing is a fiction of ideas — or rather, of one idea: change in permanence, the dynamics of equilibrium. Her early novels are important because they lay the foundations of an historical vision from which she has not yet deviated. The two poles of that vision are, on one hand, celebration of balance and cosmic order, and on the other the difficulty of men to predict, to control the "way" this order will go. Even the best of intentions may go awry, bringing about the opposite result. Each of her novels presents a "problem," an inbalance to be stabilized, things apart that must be brought together. To do so takes effort; there must be will to order, and a hero. But if this is not to become a vicious circle, a comedy of errors where each new deed only wreaks more havoc, there must be some knowledge too. In Le Guin's universe man develops as he grows wiser.

The first novel, *Rocannon's World* (1966), and to some extent the second, *Planet of Exile* (1966), are exercises in paradox. What seems insignificant, misbegotten, hopeless, turns out in the end to yield unexpected riches. As individuals, the heroes play surprisingly little part in this process. They persevere, trust in things, but have little more than a token need to trust in others, and almost none to trust in themselves. In her third novel, *City of Illusions* (1967), a significant change occurs. The battlefield shifts from the external world of stock heroic adventure to the hero's mind itself. This internalization leads to new emphases; it increases the weight of personal responsibility, and with it the possibility of human evil arising from the burden of choice, the acceptance or rejection of the limits of existence. In these early novels what is called "evil" remains primarily an external factor, the fruit of ignorance, something to be converted or destroyed. But gradually, subtly, the spectre of self-delusion grows until, in her later novels, it turns things inside out. There, instead of demonstrating that untold "good" may come from the most insignificant act, Le Guin warns that even the smallest deed, foolishly or maliciously done, can cause untold harm.

The first three Hainish novels take us from faceless enemies to a glimpse of the enemy within.

Their sequel, *The Left Hand of Darkness* (1969), completes the change; the forces of the universe no longer work on man, but through him and the institutions he creates. Le Guin's early worlds are always out-of-the-way worlds, and *Left Hand* is no different. But now this doubly isolated individual becomes the center of Le Guin's universe, responsible for achieving that inner balance which is the only base from which one man can reach out to another, fixing the bond of trust and love, and establishing the new, dynamic, human polarity of her fiction.

The early novels follow a clear sequential order. *Rocannon's World* is the story of how the League of All Worlds acquired telepathy. The hero saves his planet, and in the process becomes the first human to learn this skill. The next novel, *Planet of Exile*, is set in the League future. The inhabitants of the small Terran colony on Gamma Draconis III have the "mindspeech," but are already losing their ability to control it; faced with extinction, barbarian hordes and the onslaught of a thirty-year winter, the colony struggles to survive. Lurking behind the facade is a hint of trouble in the League. In RW, man was already arming himself against invaders from some far-off galaxy. Now something is definitely wrong; the ship the colony sent out long ago never came back. *City of Illusions*, in true sequel fashion, tells us why.

CI is the story of Falk, who emerges from mental darkness in a forest clearing, and crosses a ravaged American continent, now reduced to scattered enclaves of life. He eventually reaches the city of the Shing, rulers and enemy, in search of his identity. There he learns the Shing have been seeking him; he comes from a distant planet, and they want to know its location, presumably to destroy it. To obtain this information, they must restore his old self, and at the same time "raze" the person called Falk and all he might know of the enemy from his travels. But through an act of will, he retains the two selves, and reunites them. As Falk-Remarren, he defeats the Shing, and goes on to warn his home planet. That planet is none other than Gamma Draconis III. And finally we learn why the ship never came back. Ironically, the efforts of Jakob Agat, hero of PE, to survive on his forsaken world eventually saves the human race. From the seed he planted, a powerful culture grew up, rediscovered faster-than-light travel, and sent Remarren back to Earth.

Le Guin's saga does not follow the pathway of linear progression. No advance is permanent, no conquest stable. One thing brings about its opposite. The only certainties are balance and change. Two major themes in these novels indicate quite clearly the course of Le Guin's thought: telepathy, and the League of Worlds.

The acquisition of telepathy surprises Rocannon, for he thought his race was "deaf and blind" to it, at least in controlled form. But he soon discovers that many humans possess the potential; the Faradayan pilot, for example, is drawn to him empathically as he stands on the mountain, and the lesson nearly costs him his life. The gift brings its own burdens: "Clinging to his humanity, he had drawn back from the totality of the power . . . He had learned to listen to the minds of one race, one kind of creature: that of his enemy." To enter a mind which is ignorant of yours is to violate it. It may be done to enemies, never to friends: "Understanding must be mutual, when loyalty was, and love."

The loss of telepathic skill on the *Planet of Exile* has deep causes. Rocannon had to learn some measure of control to stay out of others' minds; the colonists on Gamma Draconis III are too much in each others minds, and are beginning to lose control. Paradoxically, to know everything about each other is to be isolated. They fear to "send," and would shut the others out; but in so doing, they cut themselves off as well. This fear is cannonized as law — it is forbidden to "send" to the natives. But Jakob Agat does project a mental warning to the Tevaran girl Rolery, saving her from the onrushing sea. This "accident" (he didn't know she was native) proves to be a very fortunate one in more ways than one, for their contact is the beginning of a chain of events which saves and unites both peoples. Telepathy is more than just a meeting of minds. The first discovery of an affinity between races thought to be biologically incompatible changes the history of the universe.

The situation in CI is far more dismal, at least initially. Men have renounced telepathy out of fear, and their masters, the Shing, have perverted it, turning an instrument of communication into one of deception, warping mindspeech into the "mindlie." Men, Falk is told, no longer use the skill because they fear the truth and have embraced the lie. With speech, there's a gap, but in telepathy contact is instantaneous, and lying is impossible. Somewhere in man's long history the bond of trust was broken, and mankind scattered; men have now reverted to the spoken word with its potential for lying and building interpersonal walls. It is also hinted that the world before the fall was not ready for telepathy, that it destroyed the art of statecraft upon which the League reposed, and left it without defense against the Shing. The Shing can mindlie; this alien quality provides them with formidable power over their human enemies. But even aliens are part of the balance, as Falk's people long ago learned on their distant planet. His "Werelians" maintain the balance by developing into skilled "paraverbalists," capable not only of detecting the lie, but of guarding their own integrity against it. They have learned to "mindguard." In an ironic twist, telepathists from a world once on the verge of slipping into the silence of egotism and barbarism are the very ones who save Earth by their skills: Falk defeats the Shing in a "mindduel." In this way he saves mankind from that "mindhandling" Rocannon first saw and recoiled from.

The course the League follows is every bit as tortuous. In *Rocannon* it is still relatively unsophisticated, an organization with imperialist overtones, operating in great haste and out of fear of some imminent danger from a far-off Enemy. On the basis of an incomplete survey, they begin tampering with the balance of things on Fomalhaut II. Their emphasis on technological development upsets this balance in ways never anticipated. Instead of preparing a barrier against enemies without, they create one within. The Faradayans themselves are too quickly developed and armed; unable to bear the moral responsibility for their new technology, they revolt and try to sieze power. Ironically, it is this blunder which finally brings man to explore the ecology of an apparently primitive planet.

Rocannon's criticism of the League is that it should first learn what minds are before it starts meddling with them. Fighting alongside the people of this world, he does just that. His is a journey through minds, from the brainless insects, the "winged ones," to the telepathic Ancient One. Rocannon's insight turns out to be prophetic in terms of the League's future, for the Enemy's weapons derive primarily from the mind. When the impersonal body fails, the individual succeeds. But the commitment must be total: Rocannon makes their world his. The gift of telepathy, of communication between minds, can only be made to one who, in exchange, gives himself.

The League of Planets has learned caution from Rocannon's experience, perhaps too much, for excessive caution can be dangerous too. In RW the hero caused a moratorium on "technical aid" to be given undeveloped worlds until further study could be made. This became the Law of Cultural Embargo: nothing is to be given to a people until they evolve to the point where they are ready for it. What the colony in Landin fails to see is that their presence on this planet is in itself a factor in the evolutionary chain. Change is inevitable, and the more they entrench themselves behind their walls and law, the harder the resistance to them becomes, and the longer and more painful the process will be. The League in RW minimized intelligent alien life forms; here its representatives come to despise them. So paths diverge until circumstances force a bloody crisis *in extremis*. The lesson learned is that "not all wisdom is written in the League Books." Breaking the law is not only inevitable, but salutary. Rolery's people never in all this time learned to make the wheel; in using these "little roundlegged boxes," she now contemplates with fresh eyes what these people take for granted and no longer see. What occurs is genuine cultural exchange. Rolery knows to wash wounds, and so saves colonists who, because they have never gotten this world's infections before, refuse to believe they are getting them now.

In *City*, the League is shattered, mankind defeated and driven apart. Ironically, Falk provides the base upon which it will be rebuilt. The bond is not forged with hominids on some strange world, but with man himself, in his own homeland. To defeat the Shing, the hero must retain his being as Falk, for only through his memories of existence on Earth could he recognize his danger. This is the one fixed point in the midst of manipulated illusion. But he can only retain his identity by wanting to. Throughout his adventures, Falk has come to love the world of man. Beneath the fear and the folly of man's actions, he has seen the dignity and imagination. At one point he stands beside his companion Estrel, who later reveals herself a Shing agent, watching the Prince of Kansas shoot firecrackers at an enemy plane passing over: "She evidently saw nothing of the lunatic, poetic dignity of those firecrackers, which ennobled even a Shing aircar with the quality of a solar eclipse. In the shadow of total calamity why not set off a firecracker?"

The reconstructed League of *Left Hand of Darkness*, the Ekumen, will emphasize communication, not political or cultural control. It is a "clearing house for knowledge" on a cosmic scale. But in the early Hainish novels, parochialism, cultural isolation, and xenophobia strike at the very heart of the League, despite its plans and laws. Without mutual understanding, fear and fanaticism take over. The Shing, the "alien," simply incarnate what is a human failing, and make it an absolute. They allow no physical contact with men; mentally they are cut off by the lie. Like Agat's colony, they too are dwindling in number; in spite of this, they would remain apart, willfully and perpetually. Their famous Law is, in reality, their means of cutting themselves off from life: "When there is no relationship, where hands do not touch, emotion atrophies in void . . . Laws are made against the impulse a people most fears in itself. *Do not kill* was the Shing's vaunted single Law. All else was permitted: which meant, perhaps, there was little else they really wanted to do. Fearing their own profound attraction towards death, they preached Reverence for Life, fooling themselves at last with their own lie." The "masters" are prisoners to their own sterile fears. In the end, however, Falk forces communication on them, taking Kenyek back with the ship: "He can tell Werel his tale about Earth, and you yours, and I mine . . . there's always more than one way to the truth."

Le Guin's "future history" differs greatly from the Heinleinian variety, where each episode is a decisive step in man's conquest of the universe. Here both man and technology are defeated; "survival of the fittest" is not a matter of guts or guile, but rather of adaptation, of knowing the limits of self and others, of reaching other minds, communicating with them but not coercing them. The rugged individuality so championed by other writers is never glorified by Le Guin. To be an individual in her universe is to be whole, and that can only happen when man accepts his responsibility as part of a balanced universe. The greater his role in that universe, the more urgent the need for understanding self and the limits of self.

Each of these three early novels celebrates balance — they are pearls on a string. In each of them two "principles" are at work — polar forces which generate and sustain their inner dynamic. The first could be called "elusiveness of control," its counterweight "fortunate paradox." What first seemed the right move, then turned out to be the wrong one, now by some unpredictable twist reveals itself to be correct after all, on another level altogether. The technique of dramatizing these intricacies of change in permanence is fully worked out in *Rocannon's World* — this is no "apprentice" piece. Later works will elaborate these techniques and explore their significance, but will not alter them in any fundamental way.

From novel to novel, mankind is growing up. As he does, more emphasis naturally falls on the individual. Balance becomes less a matter of the machine righting itself, and more a burden thrown on the hero. Rocannon is emmeshed in forces external to himself. Convention does not ask that he ponder self, but that he act. However, in *City* a shift has clearly occurred. Although this novel superficially relates a quest leading to the destruction of an unknown enemy, the difference in focus is striking. The battle cannot be fought until Falk has achieved identity: he must literally build a new self out of his divided halves. Moreover, this new, integrated self becomes the very weapon with which he fights. He lays an ambush in his mind for the unsuspecting Shing intruder, who surprises and overwhelms one personality only to be struck down unexpectedly by the other.

The principle of elusiveness of control is evident throughout *Rocannon*; "progressive" policy is folly. The troglodytes, significantly, become the chosen ones to whom the light of technology will be given; and the Cetians, who come from a cold planet, and prefer the cool darkness of cave life, are their benefactors. Rocannon disapproves of such haphazard development. But is his decision wise either? Later, when the planet is attacked, he wonders whether technology might not have prepared them better to resist. Wrong choices abound. The Faradayans cannot imagine an attack from within; all their defenses are out in space, their camp unguarded. Neither can they imagine primitive people possessing a power like telepathy. Rocannon is fooled by the clean precision of the "winged ones' " buildings, by their serene faces, the faces, obviously, of a "superior" race. But only the "rodents" of the city, the Kiemhihr, turn out to have the "humanity" to help him. No matter what his intentions, Rocannon can never control all the implications of his actions. There is no foreseeing the workings of the universe. And yet all must choose, and choice to Le Guin is clearly a form of limitation. The Fiia represent the people who "chose." They took the pastoral life of the sun, where the Clayfolk accepted the dark. But because of this, both have become "half-peoples." The Fiia know only light without dark, the Kiemhihr rather than the "winged ones." Because of this choice, the Fian Kyo's aid to Rocannon is limited: He knows his limits, and turns back.

The paradox upon which balance pivots is freedom. All men are free to choose, but choice by its very nature limits them, and only one choice can set them free — trust in one another. To pursue one's own ends we must pursue those of others. Those who ignore this Law debase themselves. The Clayfolk refusal to lend their ship to Rocannon, although they gave it over before to Semley, breaks the trust of their community. The renegade Olgyior Zagma claims he is "free," and his men their own "masters," but they are all brutal barbarians. On the opposite side is the feudal bond between Mogien and Yahan; the latter sees himself freer in such bondage than among the renegades. Mogien seeks to meet his death on grounds of his choosing, to return to his "domain." He dies saving Rocannon, and this ultimate act of freedom is the giving of one's life in self-sacrifice.

The balance which operates in *Rocannon* denies neither loss nor death. Yet the texture of the novel is woven so skillfully that we tend to see only the web, and not the holes in it. The predominance of balance is symbolized by the jewel — a thing of "dangerous beauty" — and literally traced by it. Rocannon gives the jewel three times; it is given back to him twice: the novel begins and ends with a gift. In the opening pages he gives it to Semley, the princess who came across space to claim it. Her reasons are venal: she wishes to shine as a court lady. Rocannon's gift is indifferent, a matter of colonial policy. Semley returns to find husband and court dead and gone, and pays for the stone with her sanity. Her daughter later gives it back to Rocannon, along with her son, "the greatest of gifts." Jewel and man are thus associated.. The stone is used again by Rocannon "as a ransom or a gift," not for Mogien's life, but for his servant Yahan's. Rocannon hands the jewel over with a heavy heart, and Yahan receives the benefits with equal sorrow, thereby breaking the old feudal order. But the jewel is not lost; Mogien recovers it and tosses it to Rocannon, a joking gift, "not so easily lost" as all that. Ironically, the feudal order restores itself, when Rocannon must claim Yahan as his servant to save him a second time from his master's wrath. It is significant that the stone is not offered to the Ancient One for the gift of telepathy; the gift on this occasion is Mogien's life, because telepathy draws to Rocannon the ship his friend attacks. To give the jewel entails a loss. In giving it to Semley, Rocannon follows her and loses his world as she had hers. But to give is to gain as well. In the end, the hero presents it to another blonde, Ganye, and gains a new home and wife. And he also gives himself a death, for when the ship finally comes, it finds her wearing a jewel of "mourning."

In much the same way, *Planet of Exile* is an elaborate construction of errors of judgment and fortunate turns of fate. The Terrans try very hard not to influence the natives, but change them anyway in spite of themselves. The two peoples are driven together by the Gaal invasion, and are forced to reconsider basic tenets of life: "This planning ahead, this trying to keep hold of a conquered place across both space and time, was untypical; it showed — what? An autonomous change in a hilf culture pattern, or an infection from the old northern colonies and forays of Man?" And the men are also infected by the natives, losing their immunity to the alien bacteria. But though the infections bring death, paradoxically, they also bring the promise of life, for it means that the two peoples are growing closer, both culturally and biologically. Rolery, the one born "out of season," the one never meant to bear, will be the mother of a new race. When the two communities were apart, each formed a closed circle of disharmony. Thus, Agat reasons, it is only because of their alienness, the differences between them, that they could meet across the gulf. Only in joining do they become free. The bond of love is, genetically and morally, the only possible foundation for a new future.

And as in *Rocannon*, Le Guin uses "binding" symbols to weave patterns of balance. One such symbol is the Terran cup, which matches the perfect skill of the artist with fragility of substance. To Agat, it epitomizes his people. Later in the novel, Rolery is fascinated by the same cup; like the women of the colony, it is frail-looking yet enduring. She brings to the cup a sensitivity the colonists have lost: her fresh gaze lends new life to the old marvels of Terran art. The cup becomes a tribal object, part of the ceremony of "ti" drinking. Rolery sits in the midst of this circle of drinkers, cementing the unity of the two peoples, a sharp and vivid contrast to an earlier scene which depicted the stone-pounding circle of the natives shattered by dissension. The xenophobe human Pilotson claims that her coming will destroy their order: "Jakob Agat's grandsons will sit pounding two rocks together and yelling." But in the end, Agat replaces the old native chief Wold (each has killed a snowghoul singlehandedly), and takes his place in the clan circle around the funeral pyre.

There is, in *Planet*, a certain artificiality in the use of paradox. This rage for balance comes near to bring an end in itself, the novel being reduced to almost a virtuoso piece. Le Guin may have seen this excess, and decided in her third novel to turn a vice into a virtue. *City of Illusions* displays an even more elaborate, and nearly bewildering, profusion of binding symbols and paradoxes. However, the profusion of signs serves a precise thematic function. In a novel about illusion and reality, the hero's task, like ours, is to break through the shimmering surface to truth.

Paradox thrives in CI: The Shing are rulers ruled; reverence for life is really fear of death. And the patterns of imagery are even denser. Jewels and sun, reflected light and real light, patterning frames and the frame of heaven, illusion and reality, fill the novel from its first to last pages. All are shadows to one degree or another; the clear light of truth is never seen. In the beginning, Falk reaches out for the sun, obscured in a white summer haze, as he would for a coveted jewel. Later, he is drawn by the firelight to the old Listener's cabin; and in the throneroom of Kansas, he sees an artificial sun. But even when he sees the two suns of his one lifetime, in a joyous burst of imagination, shining side by side, they nevertheless appear to him as two jewels; his vision is blurred.

No clear pattern of things ever emerges. Falk wanders around in the forest, and then on the trackless plain; he thinks he is guiding himself, but he is quite clearly being guided. Jewels abound, but they never seem to form any coherent design. Some are associated with deception, like Estrel's amulet radio. The gem city of Es Toth is a gallery of trick mirrors, a city of glass. Other jewels are linked with self-deception: the patterning frame, the glass-bead games. The search for some coherent pattern has degenerated into passivity and mysticism; practitioners "end up seeing patterns on an empty frame." Falk is the amber stone on one, the opalstone, the "jewel of luck," on another. These mysterious pronouncements are shrouded in obscurity.

As Falk's ship leaves Earth, the pattern of jewels is finally broken: "On the screen dawn coming over the Eastern Ocean shone in a golden crescent for a moment . . . like a jewel on a great patterning frame. Then frame and pattern shattered, the barrier was passed, and the little ship broke free of time and took them out across the darkness." This is more than a lyrical flourish. In the two earlier novels, the heroes could trust in patterns, even when they couldn't trust in themselves: Rocannon gives the same jewel twice to different women; the cup is a fixed point which unites Agat and Rolery. But objects in Falk's world are so elusive that he can only fall back on his inner being in his search for fixity. His companion betrays him; Orry, his countryman, may be a spy, everything in the outer world is unsure, divided. Only in Falk's mind can balance be achieved: "Against them he could never prevail except, perhaps, through the one quality no liar can cope with, integrity."

The act of will by which Rocannon breaks through to telepathy is stated purely in terms of action: "I will go south and find my enemy and destroy him." He gets his gift, and goes on to accomplish the mission. Falk's act of will, which breaks the mind-handler's hold and shatters the frame of illusion, is totally different. It is an assertion of being: "I am Falk." In later novels two things will happen. First, illusion becomes less artificial, less blatantly an illusion. The pattern becomes social creeds, religions, beliefs, rather than jewels and other tangible objects. Second, it becomes harder to break the frame or assert the self. The Shing without is easier to deal with than the Shing within. And are they as alien as they seem? As hard as they try to disguise themselves, they are probably men after all. The evil they represent is neither gratuitous nor absolute: "perhaps the essence of their lying was a profound, irremediable lack of understanding. They could not get in touch with men." There are also men who cannot get in touch with men. When the Shing becomes internalized, when fear of death masquerades as a call to eternal life, when self-delusion becomes more than an empty patterning frame, when loyalties are divided between self and world, with no total rejection or acceptance possible, then Falk's assertion is little better than Rocannon's. These early novels, however skillfully written, remain verbal skeletons, too stylized and bound by the conventions of the space adventure to be truly effective. In *The Left Hand of Darkness*, Le Guin takes a bold step, for here the Hainish saga is transposed into concrete terms — recognizable societies, with men instead of symbols.

THE LEFT HAND OF DARKNESS

The Left Hand of Darkness is far more complex than its predecessors; in terms of sheer technical skill, it is Le Guin's most satisfying work to date. A delicate balance of ideas and passions is maintained throughout. The storytelling process is intricate. Over all lies an editorial framework, intermingled with interpolated tales, documents, diaries, and constant shifts back and forth in narrative time. This richness of texture does not impede the forward movement of the story, or the sheer suspense of the main plot. The popularity of this novel — it won the Nebula and Hugo awards for best science fiction novel of 1969 — is due at least partially to a striking central idea, a world whose people are androgynous. Also, this was the first time Le Guin dealt specifically with societies as such, and attempted explicit political commentary. This book is, however, more than a trick or a trend, but a well-crafted novel in its own right. It is also part of the Hainish cycle, continuing the League saga beyond the Great War into a time of consolidation; and can only be fully understood when read in this perspective. Once again, an ethnologist-observer, Genly Ai, comes to claim a planet for the organization of worlds. The basic pattern is the same, but what Le Guin does with it is profoundly different.

The relationship of visitor to world is much more subtle in LHD. In fact, the world itself is only superficially like the others we have seen. True, it is distant, far from the center of things on Hain or Terra; it is harsh, a place where human survival is difficult; and its inhabitants are alien, in this case ambisexuals. And yet, in spite of these differences, it is a surprisingly familiar place. We recognize the political systems; their history is in many ways ours. The landscape is quite ordinary by earth standards, if a bit cold; there are no red hills or weird flora and fauna; and in fact, no animal life whatsoever. The cities are built the same way we might build them if we had to adapt to such a climate. The seasons are similar to ours. The Planet of Exile had winters thirty years long; here the planet itself is Winter, and everything is just that much colder. Finally, the aliens themselves are neither furry nor winged; they are men, but with two sexes instead of one.

This world that is almost like ours is strange by the very fact of its similarities. The experience is a profoundly alienating one to Ekumen observers. Le Guin is careful to place the problem of Gethen on a cultural and psychological level. Mankind does not "need" this world in any immediate way. The two peoples in *Planet of Exile must* unite, the stake being the continuation of the species. In *Left Hand of Darkness*, such a union is neither necessary nor probable. The result would almost certainly be sterile. Still, the possibilities are intriguing. Ekumen personnel are not forced to land on Winter; like Ai, they "choose" to do so. They represent an enlightened and open-minded civilization. Convinced they are beyond prejudice, they seek to understand — these people are men, after all. It is clear, however, that emotionally the Ekumen diplomats cannot face the implications, personal or social, of Gethenian sexuality. To reject it outright is to admit irrationality; it is easier to turn reason to unreasoning ends. They would rather demonstrate that the Gethenians don't need them. Isn't an ambisexual complete unto itself?

But Gethen does need the Ekumen. Like other planets we have seen, this one is evolving on its own. There are signs the ice may be melting. The Gethenians have not waited for fortune to change their world, but have long since adapted and conquered its cruel climate. Rugged individuality, the anarchist spirit which caused this people to survive, is no longer a necessity, and is being replaced by more collective forms of government. These changes are not wholly welcomed, for things seem to be heading in the direction of dictatorship and war. This pattern should be familiar to the Ekumen observers, who by their arrival offer a way, perhaps the only way, to avert catastrophe. Ironically, it is not the Envoy who sees the need, or who realizes the importance of what he brings. It is a "native," the statesman Estraven of Karhide.

But why is the Ekumen so blind? They are not only older and wiser than the earlier League, but more thorough as well — there are no more incomplete surveys like the one on Rocannon's world. The sexual nature of the Gethenians seems an insurmountable barrier to understanding. According to the observer who studies the social implications of this androgyny, neither aggressiveness nor war is possible in their society. They are neither man nor woman, but only "potentials," in "kemmer" (heat) once a month, never knowing beforehand which role they will play. The rest of the time they live in a society without sex and its attendant frustrations.

And yet they are heading for war. A people who achieved industrial society without an "industrial revolution" are finding other frustrations to replace sexual ones. But the observers seem incapable of learning from them. This sexless society seems a libber's dream come true, but the woman from Chiffewar, the observer, is "appalled" at the thought of being treated, not as a woman, but merely as a "human being." They are just enough like us that we cannot look at them objectively and respect them for their differences. Like *City*, this novel is about illusion, a different and far more dangerous kind than that which beset Falk. It cuts to the core of our being, of our capacity for tolerance and adaptibility. To say that the Gethenians might be the result of a Hainish "experiment" that failed is one last, most devious and desperate attempt to exorcise the demon. But the common root, humanity, returns in the guilt that haunts them. Ai's task as the observer who comes to adopt the ways and customs of an alien people is made doubly arduous. In the face of this formidable psychological barrier, he will have to learn that the alien, like man, is capable both of aggression and love.

Left Hand confronts men with viable, living societies. The vague, impersonal forces represented in the earlier books — nature in the raw or barbarian hordes — are still present, but play a secondary role before the precise social mechanisms of Winter. Some critics have spoken of a disparity between public and private "imperatives" in the novel: for the first time in Le Guin's work, union between men and the fixing of a bond of mutual trust are no longer automatically the basis for restored harmony in the public sphere. The same thing is true for the union within, Falk balances himself and saves a world. Estraven's life is perhaps rounded out with a love, but his banishment and disgrace remain. Ai too, after the conquest of of the ice, after forging a bond with Estraven and with nature, must return to diplomacy to inconclusive bargaining. The ship is brought down; one wonders, however, whether this will bring any lasting order to the political mess.

Le Guin is not competing with Orwell or Hemingway. Her social analysis is acute, but its purpose is not indignation or reform. She has no social program, offers no panaceas. Nor does she, at the other extreme, give us characters who turn their backs on seemingly hopeless social chaos, and go off to the wilderness to carve some private relationship out of confrontation with the elements. Ai and Estraven are forced by society to cross the ice; there is no other way. They do not flee one society to return to another (both are inadequate), nor do they take refuge in each other. Paradoxically, they make their journey to renew society, but on a deeper level, at the roots.

What constitutes the public world in *Left Hand*? Orgoreyn is a "socialist" system which dehumanizes its citizens. Karhide is a comic opera kingdom which, following the example of its neighbor, is moving toward greater centralization under dictatorship. Asked if he hates Orgoreyn, Estraven says he would "rather be in Karhide." He does not understand an abstraction like "patriotism;" love of one's country is not hate of one's uncountry. To Estraven, Karhide is not a government but a place, and a better one only because it is closer to the basic realities of his culture and world. And yet, despite differences in governments, both nations share common roots; the deeper stratum of custom, myth, religious practice is the true public world of Gethen. Its institutions are reflected not in monarchy and socialism, nor even in anarchism, but in Handdara "fastness" and *shifgrethor*, the "pride relationship" between individuals which shapes everyday life on the planet. Both Estraven and Ai make a journey to the East (Orgoreyn), and find that the high point of this "progressive" nation is, ironically, the concentration camp. The way back to Karhide is over the ice, that same ice which lies at the heart of myth and legend on this cold world. Their struggle is not just a journey to Karhide. Rather it is a quest for sources, discovery of the roots of this strange culture, a culture where individual achievement and the brother-bond remain the soul that moves the collective body.

The theme of roots and rootlessness is central to Le Guin's work. It has grown steadily in importance from novel to novel, culminating in the recent confluence of three favorite images — tree, root and dream (in *The Word for World Is Forest* the word for "dream" is the same as that for "root"). This combined imagery lends a certain universality to her work that was never before present. From the start, her heroes have invariably been aliens of one sort or another, cut off from their roots. The mechanics of near-lightspeed travel do this very nicely — Genly Ai is such a rootless one, family and friends all wiped out in the "jump." Estraven, on the other hand, is banished by Karhide; we learn later that he has been cut off from much deeper familiar roots. These drifting heroes invariably seek (and generally find) new roots. Rocannon discovers them in rather flimsy feudalism; Falk, the twice-exiled, finds them in his own mind and being. The difference with Estraven is that the roots he seeks are genuinely collective, those of his race and culture. "Insofar as I love life, I love the hills of Estre" (the place which gave him his name and took it from him as well). Estraven follows the Handdara in rejecting abstractions, in holding fast to the thing or object. Making contact with this world, Ai is led astray by surfaces; illusion fills Karhide, perversion corrupts Orgoreyn. But if, as Ai says, the Ekumen must reach these people's "sense of humanity" to establish any real contact, he must start with the man; neither clowns nor zombies will do. And with Estraven he goes to the roots.

At work in *Left Hand* is an intricate system of paradoxes: limits are freedom, freedom represents limits. To move in a circle is to progress; to progress is to return to move in a circle. Estraven seems to get nowhere in his political efforts, to be going in circles; but on another deeper path he is moving toward something of great public significance. His conservative return to the roots turns out to be the most revolutionary, far-seeing act in the novel. Circumstances in the social realm do not limit or prevent human contact between himself and Ai, they bring it about. Before his ordeal on the ice, Estraven was devoted mainly to an ideal; on the glacier, he becomes friend and companion to a man.

Things are not what they first seem. The wondrous balance of the earlier novels, which became almost an end in itself, has shifted. Individual man is placed squarely at the center of LHD; he must not only discover the fundamental rhythms of life, but commit himself to them and work toward equilibrium. Men are responsible for upsetting the balance; the visionary seeks to right it. Thus, Estraven sees, while Ai, the professional observer, is blind.

Vision is necessary to penetrate the complex patterns of imagery in this novel. Light and darkness, shadow and snow, are things of constantly shifting valence, ambiguous, inscrutable, and yet essential. They are not mere bindings — one follows Rocannon's jewel like a bouncing ball. This time they are interwoven solidly into the fabric of Gethen's institutions and culture. Ambiguity is no shimmering surface, a frame of illusion to be shattered; on the contrary, freedom lies, if anywhere, in embracing it. Nor is it a sign of nature's indifference to man. It is, rather, the ambiguity of a world order which, for man's ultimate salvation, defies that simple moral interpretation which would make white a "good" or an "evil." It is an order of primary substances which resist man's attempts to preempt or enclose them in systems, ideologies, or religious principles. In LHD, the heroes come in contact with the bases of things — cold, warmth, ice, visible darkness.

Estraven is the key to his world, the follower of circles and the breaker of circles. Caught in the circle of Karhide and Orgoreyn, he dies, and in dying, breaks out to the Ekumen, to a higher order of things. He is also, apparently, captive to the circle of his fated love — the path across the ice has been taken before by his exiled brother-lover. Estraven draws Ai into the circle, and in so doing, breaks it. His lover and brother are restored to him, but in the form of the stranger from space; the act which brings freedom is in itself a new binding. Estraven's personal roots lie in the two true institutions of Gethen: as a statesman, he is master of *shifgrethor*; by birth and discipline, he is an adept of the Handdara. In reaching out to Ai, embracing his cause, he must break loose from these as well, from his own culture. What he discovers is another circle, one of interplanetary magnitude: the stranger's culture, so apparently different on the surface, has deep affinities with his own.

Estraven tells Ai that *shifgrethor* comes from an old word meaning "shadow." In its most elementary form, it is the point at which each individual intersects social reality, and attains his "status." This status is not rank, but its opposite, the ability to maintain equality in any relationship, and to do so by respecting the person of the other. When Ashe, the fallen minister's "kemmering," approaches Ai, to take money to Estraven in Orgoreyn, he plays *shifgrethor*. He neither begs nor orders, but throws the burden of obligation on Ai by appealing to his pride in self. Instead of a draft in Estraven's name, he gives Ai cash; there is nothing to incriminate him if caught, and nothing to prevent him from spending the money himself. The Ortoga have perverted this principle. In another scene, King Argaven thinks the Envoy mad; but he never questions his integrity: as one madman to another, he believes him. In Orgoreyn, Ai is taken for a liar. Fear negates life; out of fear of being hoaxed, the easterners deny Ai being. But in violating his shadow, they destroy their own. To Ai, they seem to cast no shadow at all, and what casts no shadow has no substance.

In his dealings with Ai, Estraven must give up his shadow. The Envoy, whose concept of personal pride apparently is totally different, misconstrues everything Estraven tells him. The ultimate act of *shifgrethor* is to abandon it: "He is infinitely a stranger, and I a fool, to let my shadow cross the light of the hope he brings us." Held too long, the shadow can become "mortal vanity." But a man's shadow may also become his name and his reputation. Estraven gives this all up when he embraces Ai's cause. Finally, the shadow is a man's death. Mogien, in *Rocannon*, saw the shadow of his own passing, and went to meet it freely. Estraven trades his life for this new light of hope.

Shifgrethor is perhaps in a deeper sense another sort of projection, off of darkness. The Gethenians call it a "sublimination" of man's primitive fears and anger, a "refinement" man erects over chaos. The new minister of Karhide, Tibe, abandons *shifgrethor*, seeking in his demagoguery to drag his people back into the morass of elemental disorder, hoping to "unite" them by destroying their individuality. In this he follows the lead of Orgoreyn. Tired of the confusion in Karhide, Ai goes to Orgoreyn, and is pleased at first with its clean, neat appearance, the well-tended fields and rational cities. He soon learns how void this is. The real Orgoreyn is the darkness below — the cellar of his first night, the cattle car in which he is deported. The people of the land are walking shades, with drugged bodies and programmed minds. In a neat *contrapasso* they have become shadows of darkness.

Once again, man's will is the main factor — he can succumb to darkness or create something out of it. The primeval chaos of night can be fecund as well as destructive, the source of light as well as gloom, according to the central beliefs of the old Handdara religion, which still flourishes in Karhide, but has been supplanted by a new sect in Orgoreyn. Its basis is the saying: "Praise darkness and creation unfinished." In the Handdara "fastness" ceremony, a "weaver" brings light out of the darkness of madness, perversion, and sexual frustration. In this "foretelling," the moment of answer is a closing of the broken circle. What the light reveals is the truth of uncertainty. The word "foretelling" is ironic: all that is learned is what questions *not* to ask.

Such wisdom is not enough for Orgoreyn; they must have light. Significantly, their cult is born of a breaking asunder of the "fastness" circle. The unanswerable question, "what is the meaning of life?" ends in violence and murder. Faith deifies Meshe the man; he is the "all-seeing," who denies darkness, and reviles all who consider it source and end. This classic sect, complete with priests and oaths, is perfect for a police state, where nothing should go unseen. But to deny darkness is to deny change, the dynamic polarity at the core of existence. In refusing death, they refuse life as well. According to the Karhiders (whose saving grace is their humor), this cult seeks to enshrine its founder — none other than the "weaver" of that broken circle — in a vacuum at the moment he receives the "answer," so that he will shine forever. There may not be an answer, or much life, but there is light — from a lightbulb.

The light that emanates from the Handdara "weaver" is also heat, the substance of life. Meshe's light is cold; and Ai, in Orgoreyn, experiences heat that does not warm, comforts that do not satisfy. On the other hand, although Winter is an icy world, there is fire at its heart — up through the glaciers volcanoes spout flame. This ice may seem, in itself, the absolute denial of life and warmth. Yet in the "pre-Yomesh" creation myth life itself is created from melting ice. And it is the white cold of the ice-world that drives Ai and Estraven into the warmth of human solidarity inside their lonely tent. Further, the "white weather" seems to be the light that takes life, and robs men of even their shadows. Ironically, however, the inconceivable union of two so alien may be due precisely to this loss of image: stripped of their shadows, they discover how small their differences really are. They are created anew, and see anew.

The ambiguity present in this book is the true state of things, according to Le Guin. Only in complexity does balance function; to simplify this process, or elevate one factor above all others, is to disturb the ongoing dynamic. Like the actions of the Shing, it is undoubtedly the result of profound misunderstanding. But here, in the world of real states and governments, ignorance is quickly perverted into a most tenacious evil. Meshe is not just blind; he also forces others to believe that he sees. The Ortoga are not merely incredulous; they show Ai a *will* to incredulity. In *Left Hand* man is put to the proof, and he shows us how serious his undoings can be. But if man takes things beyond the point where they can right themselves, then the only thing that can ever correct them is another man. The responsibility for order is henceforth in his hands. Estraven finds this task, his life's work, extraordinarily difficult. Where Rocannon simply followed his calling, Estraven must pass through a labyrinth of political intrigue. Wit is not enough to carry him forward; he must also have another guide, the muse Ai invokes at the beginning of his tale — imagination.

Truth, says Ai is merely a matter of imagination in his story.

And bold leaps are required of Estraven throughout. The dangers of boldness are clearly stated in the tale of Estraven's ancestors, where a blood feud between rival houses is resolved by a daring act of love. The fruit of this union becomes, in turn, the cause of new dissension; his very being has usurped the right of succession of the other "hearth-brothers." They turn on him, and he kills them in battle. Both for ending the feud *and* for this killing of brothers, we are told, this earlier Estraven was called "traitor." The first accusation may be ignored as reactionary. But what of the second? In creating one balance, another is upset.

The rhythm of the Handdara "fastness" is double: one breaks through chaos to light, but that light is of necessity impermanent. Life is only possible because there is "permanent intolerable uncertainty." Men like the Yomeshta, who deify their singularity, are "ecology-breakers." Is there not an opposity malady — a despair born of this permanence of change? Estraven's genius is to thread a way between these two pitfalls. His world is not, he sees, "one fastness of the Handdara . . . alas we must walk forward troubling the new snow, proving and disproving, asking and answering." The one truth is that things go forward; and though it is hazardous to try to plot the way, man must attempt it nevertheless.

But how should we judge Estraven's final act then — his death? Ai at first thinks it suicide; Estraven could have avoided it. To this culture suicide is the denial of forgiveness, change, and life. Estraven may sometimes speak in terms which sound fatalistic ("I was born for exile . . . my one way home is by way of dying"), but is he a fatalist? The tale of Herbor and Berosty — another love story — is an old style "fate tragedy" which contrasts significantly with Estraven's career. Here the obsession with fate is itself a form of suicide; in the paralyzing fear which results from trying to foresee the details of one's destiny, love and life are denied. He who would outwit his fate meets it all the more surely in the end, with his wasted life in between. Estraven is not interested in the end — the one thing all men are sure of is death. What counts is life; here he is free, and he chooses to give his life to Ai and his cause. Ai has forgotten what he said as the two men embarked on that apparently impossible trek across the ice: "It is good to have an end to journey towards, but it is the journey that matters in the end . . . we put on our skis and took off, down . . . into that silent vastness of fire and ice that said in enormous letters of black and white DEATH . . . the sledge pulled like a feather and we laughed with joy." So Estraven skis into the guns of the guards.

Left Hand of Darkness is less a novel of heroism than of love. Genly Ai, the narrator-observer, is the stranger in a strange land. The character of Ai is adapted from the old travel narrative tradition; he represents the visitor from a "superior" culture who is actually quite naive. The fact that he comes from an old culture does not spare him the necessity of growing up. If the Ekumen is not a government but a form of "education," then its envoy must do just that — be formed. The Ekumen sends one man; their mode of action is his personal experience. This is the theory; the planet Winter turns out to be a hard test for it, and for Ai.

Ai at first expounds the Ekumen theory haughtily: "The Ekumen could not appeal to these people as a social unit . . . it must speak to their strong though underdeveloped sense of humanity." But to say "we are all men" is somewhat like Meshe saying everything is light: it denies differences. He must learn, the hard way, that differences must be recognized and accepted before any real common ground can be reached. The Gethenians may be men, but they are also, as Estraven sees, profoundly different. Ai must also learn that seeking common ground is a path of no return; both parties are altered in the process. Ai says: "Alone I cannot change your world. But I can be changed by it." Again he is right, and again wrong. He does indeed change, more than he ever would have imagined, but in changing he changes things too, perhaps a whole world. Ai at first sees very little. He dismisses Karhide, not seeing that though its people are "out of step," they are still marching together, and perhaps form more of a society than one that goosesteps. He cannot know a people till he knows an individual among them, until he meets Estraven at the heart of the storm.

The meaning of Ai's name has fascinated the critics. Obviously, he represents an "I," an ego who accomplishes his being only when he enters into the most personal of relationships with Estraven: "I and Thou." Some have also seen him as an "eye," the observer-become-actor. On the ice, Estraven comes to see his name quite differently — it is a cry of pain. There is more "basic humanity" in his name than in all his speeches, for pain is the human condition; and as the two share their suffering on the glacier, they cease to be alien to one another. Ai comes all the way to this strange place to learn what it is to be a man. Ironically, in becoming himself he becomes part of the alien world, a brother to Estraven, linked with the deepest currents of his culture, and destined to carry on the vision of its greatest statesman.

Ai makes wrong judgments from the start, and his worst is of Estraven: "I am the only man in Gethen who trusted you entirely, and I am the only one in Gethen you refused to trust." But could it have been otherwise? Up to now Estraven has misunderstood his man too. Not even he, at this moment before the ice, realizes what the cost of mutual trust might be. When he says (half-jokingly): "Teach me your mindspeech, the language that has no lies in it, and then ask me why I did what I've done," he cannot imagine the price of such a bond. The mindspeaking episode is the center of their experience on the ice, and follows a gradual, natural breakdown of barriers between the two men. First the sexual barrier falls: in realizing how alone Estraven's race can be on this world empty of other living species, in seeing that ambisexuality, self-sufficiency, might also become loneliness, the envoy realizes that he is not the only one alone in the universe. Only then does he see that women are even more alien to him than Estraven, with whom he shares at least one sex part of the time. The barrier of pride falls too. Ai gives Estraven mindspeech because he wants to: "I had simply arrived at the point where we shared whatever we had that was worth sharing." The love that results is possible only because Ai can now respect the other's reality, and accept him as he is. With love, he must also accept responsibility for pain: he had never before realized that he could hurt Estraven.

At one point Estraven says: "How shall we deal with strangers, except as brothers." This transformation literally comes to pass in the mindspeaking episode. When Ai speaks in his mind, he whispers with the voice of Estraven's long dead brother — and he calls him by his true name, Therem. Estraven now feels the pain of words lightly spoken, as he recounts his fateful past, and his star-crossed love. His brother had been his one true love: "The only true vow of faithfulness I ever swore was not spoken, nor could it be spoken, and the man I swore it to is dead and the promise broken, long ago." Even in this androgynous world, incest is limited, and love can be tragic. In the face of this terror, Estraven goes on to "bespeak" Ai. The Envoy sees it as proof of his "insatiable, outreaching mind." But it is far more than that, a supreme act of love, one Ai can only begin to fathom. At this moment, he learns a profound truth about human communication: the light he brings serves only to measure the vastness of the dark below.

The darkness of Estraven's past is deep, but from such depths comes hope. The story of the "place inside the blizzard" reveals the tragic tale of two brother-lovers and their ill-fated union. The pair refuse to part, but social strictures drives one to suicide, and the vow is broken anyway. The remaining brother must go into exile, give up his name as a curse upon his house, and journey to the "white place" inside the storm. Here he meets his dead brother again, but the encounter is futile, as the suicide cannot call his name. This pattern could also be Estraven's, right down to the "meeting" with his own dead brother (also a suicide?), in the same white world where none cast shadows or have names. The hold of the past, of custom and racial law, is suspended by the new act of mind-speech. The speaker, though alien, is a living man, not some shade of a suicide; the name is spoken. The "traitor" recovers his true name from the stranger, and the broken vow is, in a sense, sealed anew. Estraven may return to Karhide and his death, but he is no longer really an exile in the deeper sense. The thrust of the novel is not merely private; Ai and Estraven tap the roots of legend and myth with their mindspeech, and alter them. Nothing is fixed forever; things go forward in the most unexpected ways.

It is only with Estraven's death that Ai begins to see into the depths of darkness, and to understand the meaning and extent of Estraven's love. As the latter lies dying in the snow, he calls out to Ai with the name of his dead brother. What was forced on him has apparently been fully accepted. But if Ai has become his brother, the Envoy must accept in turn the responsibilities it brings. At the beginning of the novel, Estraven explained to him the custom of cementing a keystone with mortar mixed with blood. Now the blood has been shed; it falls to Ai to carry out Estraven's dream: "I must set the keystone in the arch." Hopefully the space ship is that stone.

Ai's final voyage to Estraven's hearth shows him that things are beyond recall — he is alone. At the same time, it reveals just how much a part of Estraven and his world he had become. The old father introduces him to his "sons' son," and in a flash, he sees what he could only have suspected before. The nature of his own relationship with Estraven shifts again in his perceptions. But the boy remains, keystone of an arch cast long before his coming, and Ai is a stranger once more. Where is his home now? Like Gulliver returned from the Houyn-hmhms, he watches his own people step from their spacecraft, and feels estranged. Ai gave them up for Estraven, and now he is gone too. What does remain, however, is their common ordeal. When the father asks him to relate the story of the ice, he has become (like Estraven before him) a teller of tales, and a legend on this world.

The earlier novels ended on a note of hope for the human race. Whatever losses were sustained were recoverable in the balance. *Left Hand* ends with a different mood. There is no "jewel of mourning," no epic funeral. What remains is a tale, and the imperfection of human friendship in the inconclusive world of man's affairs. To accomplish his end, Ai must accept the betrayal of his promise to Estraven — his name goes uncleared. What is worse, he must continue for his friend's sake to delude himself. To Estraven's father he tells the merciful lie: "Therem was no traitor. What does it matter what fools call him?" But the old man knows it matters, and so does Ai, for Estraven is dead. True, the Ekumen's way seems to have conquered. But wasn't it always there? Didn't Ai point out to his friend that both worlds have their Yin and Yang? By the same token, there are also men in both places who refuse to respect this balance, and who willfully seek to upset it. In LHD, the enemy within has proven itself far more dangerous than the enemy without. No one in the book is without his folly or misunderstanding. And there is more than a whiff of some stronger, more stubborn perversion in man.

Finally, there is death. It is not so easily subsumed into the order of things here. Estraven is a "shadow on snow." Snow may melt to form new life, but the shadow of the man has disappeared. Ai's question: "Why must he die?" continues to echo to the end of this novel. Of all the unanswerables, it is most troubling.

THE EARTHSEA TRILOGY

The *Earthsea Trilogy* has generally been ignored by commentators on Le Guin. Some may have been deterred by the silly publishing classification which designates the books as "children's literature." More likely, though, the trilogy has simply seemed a world apart, self-contained, obeying the laws of the high fantasy genre, and having little in common with the Hainish "mainstream." Such logic may apply to writers whose world view is incoherent or inconsistent, but not to Le Guin. *Earthsea* does stand apart to the extent that it forms a carefully balanced whole. But, more essentially, it creates a universe which is parallel to that of the Hainish novels, one in which major themes are not simply mirrored or reflected, but carried forward and developed in new ways. The problems of individual responsibility, of folly, evil and the search for selfhood, are examined throughout these books in all their purity.

The first novel in the series, *A Wizard of Earthsea*, was published in 1968, one year before *Left Hand of Darkness*. The second, *The Tombs of Atuan*, appeared in 1971, slightly before *The Lathe of Heaven*, a work in which Le Guin abandons the Hainish world for a contemporary one, Portland, Oregon of the not-too-distant future. It is hard to imagine two books more different. The last Earthsea novel, *The Farthest Shore* (1972), came out the same time as the long novella,

The Word for World Is Forest. Here again, in appearance at least, are two widely divergent books, one set in a beautifully realized world of purest epic fantasy, the other in a thinly disguised Vietnam of the future. The period between *Left Hand* and the publication of the next major Hainish novel, *The Dispossessed* (1974), seems one of experimentation and turmoil. Actually, it is one of bifurcation: on one hand, Le Guin pursues the intricacies of balance in a fantasy setting which bears no resemblance whatever to our contemporary world; on the other, she examines the need to come to grips with the problems of the day, to take the Hainish epic — whose cultural high point is reached in LHD — back beyond *Rocannon* to its barbaric, American past.

For Le Guin, *Left Hand* is a crossroads. In that novel, evil is less an individual will to power than a collective one. This vision apparently gives rise to a series of works in which social systems are the villains, the disrupters of balance. Captain Davidson in *Word* is not an individual but a type — the tool of the exploitative capitalist society he represents. Even the power-mad Dr. Haber in *Lathe* is only the incarnation of a sort of liberal reformism familiar to us all. There are, however, both individuals and societies in *Left Hand*. In Ai's youthful arrogance, in the pride that brings him to misunderstand Estraven and his world, we see the potential for a much different approach to the problem of evil. It is this emphasis on man's growing awareness of the capacity for evil within him, that is developed in *Earthsea*. Neither Ged the Hero, nor his adversary, Cob the Unmaker, represent anything but themselves; what they serve or disserve directly is the Equilibrium. And they are responsible, ultimately, to themselves alone.

The Dispossessed will mark a return to more subtle interplay between society and the individual. In redressing this balance, the role of *Earthsea* is not to be minimized. During these experimentive years, it provided a counterweight to what was otherwise an excess of pessimism. Le Guin appears to have been swept along by the results of the Vietnam War; her indictment of our own destructive evil, the technocratic state and the machine without individuals, is impassioned and yet too simplistic at the same time. Le Guin herself, in an afterword to *Word*, sees the danger of being driven by a "boss" dictating to her, of moral considerations usurping artistic ones: "But the boss wanted to talk about the destruction of eco- logical balance and the rejection of emotional balance. He didn't want to play. He wanted to moralize. I am not very fond of moralistic tales, for they often lack charity." And in actual fact, this tale sounds a new note of despair. The seed of evil has been sown in Edenic "New Tahiti"; its people now know how to kill one another. And this world is not claimed by the League, but abandoned to its own destiny. After ravag- ing it, man has but one alternative left — to leave it alone. In another story from this period, "Vaster than Empires and More Slow," the hero chooses mystical union with a sentient forest world over human society, the unity of this vegetable being is preferable to the mental chaos of his fellow men, to whom his empathic powers give him access. Here is a colonist of one, a man who goes over to the "enemy" and abandons mankind. During this period of Le Guin's career, only the Earthsea books prove the value of positive individual action. The three novels celebrate the ability of one man, Ged, to overcome his pride and fear, and defeat an adversary who has succumbed to both, and then, from the base of his heroic combat, to project a new society of peace and justice to re- place the old world of disunity and violence.

The difference between the Earthsea novels and the others of the same period is, most fundamentally, one of style. In an essay written in 1973, "From Elfland to Poughkeepsie," Le Guin talks about writing fantasy stories: one's writing style, she says, should be neutral, with few modernisms or archaisms sprinkled in; it should attempt to create a world never before seen in the clearest, most direct language possible. "In fantasy there is nothing but the writer's vision of the world. There is no borrowed reality of history, or current events . . . There is no comfortable matrix of the commonplace to substitute for the imagination, to provide ready-made emotional response . . . To create what Tolkien calls 'a secondary universe' is to make a new world. A world where no voice has ever spoken before." Fortunately, voices have spoken before in the world of Earthsea. But the voices are those of myth, of the epic tradition itself. Through its language, the trilogy purifies and starts anew. But though they avoid the harsh "Poughkeepsie" speech of the Davidsons and Habers, the books do not avoid moral degradation, nor do they mitigate the power of evil. *Earthsea* is a work of high style and imagination. *The Farthest Shore* is a work of genuine epic vision.

Ged is a fully developed hero, and interestingly, one of a new sort. Le Guin's earlier heroes were scientists or statesmen. Ged is a "mage." In her essay, "Dreams Must Explain Themselves" (1973), Le Guin tells us her mage is an artist — the trilogy is an artist-novel. Traditionally, the artist is the most private of heroes; the struggle to create is primarily a struggle with self, with one's own powers and the need to control them and their consequences. The scientists and "observers" of earlier novels occupy an intermediate position between men of action and the artist. But in Le Guin the pull is always toward action. Both Rocannon and Genly Ai are drawn into an active role through contact with a man of action. Ged is a loner. *Wizard* tells the story of a private battle; the two books which follow show the hero moving toward companionship and collaboration. The quest in *Farthest Shore*, though undertaken in the same secretive, unassuming spirit as always, has profound public implications. The artist no longer travels alone; and the one he takes with him is not another mage, but a young prince, trained not in the arts, but with the sword. Le Guin's portrait of the artist looks forward, in a sense, to her new hero, Shevek, in *The Dispossessed*. Shevek is the scientist with an artist's temperament, the creative genius. Ged learns that, although the magician is safe on Roke, the wizard's school, real creation begins only when he has left the ivory tower and gone forth into life. Shevek also sees that he cannot simply formulate a revolutionary theory, and send out the book containing it. He must also go with it, and fight for his ideas, assuming public responsibility for his act of genius.

In "Dreams Must Explain Themselves," Le Guin describes the thematic progression of the three Earthsea novels. *Wizard* deals with the hero's "coming of age." It is a novel of initiation and apprenticeship. The subject of *Tombs* is "sex"; it relates a "feminine coming of age." In broader terms, its theme is love. The third novel, *Farthest*, is about death, "a coming of age again," says Le Guin, "but in a larger context." This is the hero's last and greatest adventure. First an apprentice, then a master, Ged-grown-old now takes a new apprentice with him, thus completing the epic chain. The adventure is also, in a way, a return. Young Ged became a man by accepting and absorbing the shadow of his own death. Now he goes to fight a man who has refused death, who has been possessed by his shadow.

The central theme of all these novels is the nature of human evil. The exploration takes place within the same limits as always: the universe is still a creative, dynamic balance, Yin and Yang, not a Manichean contention between light as good and darkness as evil. Evil is still explicable as a misunderstanding of the dynamics of life. What has become awesome, however, is the power one man, each man, wields, potentially and actually, to disrupt the balance. The setting in *Left Hand* is realistic; here it can only be called allegorical. Ged is both an ideal hero in an idealized world order, and an everyman. His powers seem exceptional, and yet he wins his greatest battles with means we all possess. *Earthsea*, in its sharp, limited vision, explores in depth the question of individual responsibility. To deny death is to turn from life. But worse still is to project an anti-shadow, abstracting personal fear into a general virtue, and making fear of death into a quest for eternal life.

The image of the shadow dominates *Wizard*, as it does *Left Hand*. Like all of Le Guin's heroes, Ged is an alien, an orphan in the spiritual sense, ignored by his insensitive parent. Like the odd ones of myth and fairy tale, this child of innate gifts is sired by ordinary people. The "mage born" is adopted by the wizard Ogion and made his apprentice. But in his god-given gift lie the dangers of pride and ambition, and to these Ged succumbs. His attempt to raise the dead, to prove his power through an unnatural act, looses the terrible shadow upon him. He had been warned by Ogion that danger surrounds power as shadow surrounds light. Like all men, Ged must learn his limitations the hard way, and bear the consequences of his act. These consequences, fortunately, also have their limits; if it were not so, the balance would have long since failed. Young Ged is foolish, not wicked; but he releases a force which nonetheless seeks to possess him, to turn him into an instrument of evil. The novel narrates his struggle with the shadow — first his attempts to flee, then his resolve to hunt it down, and finally his confrontation and victory.

But what is the nature of Ged's struggle? The enemy is a shadow, part of the hero himself, something from within. And, yet, Ged moves in a world where things seem to be working against him, leading him to ruin. He is pursued by a hostile destiny. It is the young witch girl on Gont who, daring Ged, first suggests raising the dead. This leads him to read the fatal runes in Ogion's book. Jasper again dares him — and this time he raises the dead, and releases the shadow with it. Then there is the mysterious messenger who directs him to Osskil, where the shadow nearly takes his life. These figures exist — we see and hear them. But as "antagonists," they too are shadows, of Ged's own mind. He comes close at one point to believing in fate. This is more than illusion; Ged is fooling himself. For in seeking "causes" outside of himself, he avoids the look within. His own pride and fear have invested neutral shapes with purpose and hostile will in an attempt to cast the weight of responsibility onto something beyond him. In the final episode on the open sea, the man is alone with his shadow. Before he finally absorbs it, it changes shape. What passes before him is his own life. One of the shapes is Jasper; but he also sees his father, and Pechvarry his friend. The shadow is formed of his own acts and choices, and in accepting it, he accepts responsibility for them. For he, not Jasper or any other man or force, must bear the blame for what he does.

At first reading, the mood cast by *Wizard* is strange and dream-like; we seem to fluctuate between objective reality and the hero's mind. The shadow is loosed into a very real world — an Archmage dies sealing the breach — but is gradually drawn back towards Ged. The hero's adversaries are sometimes phantoms of his own creation, and sometimes real powers, like the dragons and the Lord of Terrenon. Behind this fluctuation lies a carefully controlled pattern. The traditional novel of apprenticeship shows the hero first learning, then doing. But Ged is the sorcerer's apprentice — he does before he learns, and his first deed is misbegotten. For this mistake he is not sequestered; instead he becomes a mage, and is sent forth, master of his craft, but still ignorant of its implications. Again and again, life forces him to act first and learn later. Confronting the problem of action, he comes to see a deeper truth: to do great deeds, one must be whole oneself. And one is whole only by knowing one's limits.

Ged learns that what is done counts less than the spirit in which it is done. Tired of waiting in fear on the archipelago where he has become mage, Ged goes recklessly forward to brave the dragon, hoping to force the shadow into the open. But along with these private motives goes a public duty — he goes to prevent the dragons from invading his islands. Though he defeats the worm, it comes close to defeating him in turn. He has won the right to one mastery, one only. The dragon tempts him by offering the name of the thing that pursues him. Ged does not fail the archipelago, but the choice is painful. Self has gotten in the way of the deed, and the gift cannot be given freely. The Stone of Terrenon tempts him too in the same way, with that illusive name. To know something's true name is to have power over it. Ged realizes that one can act freely, without reservations, only when such temptation is put aside. To do so, he must accept in himself the thing whose name he seeks — death. The hardest task for Ged is not the heroic deed; it is the act of mind which necessarily denies his exceptional nature, and places him on a level with all the rest — the acceptance of his common mortality. What he has begun, all men begin and finish — their lives.

But what is the nature of evil in *Wizard*? What does the symbolism of darkness signify? Earthsea contains many "dark powers" — the Stone of Terrenon, the dragons. But these are primeval, inhuman powers; beside them and over them man has built up civilization. The use of the Old Speech, for instance, binds a man to truth, but dragons can twist true words to false ends, because this language is theirs. These true-namers are fundamentally indifferent to man, they are un-man. In order to exist, man must strike a balance with them. They cannot be conquered, but they must be contained: Ged names and fixes the dragon, and the stone is sealed in the fortress. They must not be served, because, in seeking to rule these forces, man enslaves himself to them — he consents to darkness. In the same way, Ged, wishing to rule over death by his conjuring, consents to it, and so becomes its prey.

But just what is this "shadow" he releases? Does it represent Death, a figure that walks among us; or is it a figure of his mind, the "shadow of his own death"? Ged flees the shadow, and it nearly claims him. Is he the victim of his own fears? The Otak dies to remind us that the struggle is not entirely in the mind. Ged pursues the shadow, and runs aground, nearly perishing. Finally, he stops running or searching; he knows that neither can escape their fate. When they have finally come to the time and the place destined for their last meeting, then they will meet. This other is Death, but the hero does not meet it here. But what does he encounter on the sand inside the ocean? The place is nowhere if not in the mind. And the act is inconclusive in terms of conquest or defeat: Ged neither loses nor wins, but in naming the shadow of his death with his own name, he makes himself whole again as a man. The evil here is neither death nor the darkness; it is rather Ged's refusal to grant these things their rightful place in the balance of nature. Only the whole man, who has accepted death, is free to serve the powers of life. Yet for all of this, Le Guin does not intend death to lose its sting or its reality. The ambiguity of the shadow is purposeful, for it reminds us that the mind is not everything. Death is, as Ged affirms in a moment of gloom, more than fear or a misunderstanding of life. It is a power as well, perhaps the only one that has any real hold on man.

It is significant that the struggle with the shadow is not mentioned in the epic poem celebrating the mage's life, whereas the journey to the tombs is. The first merely lays the foundation for deeds, the second is the true public act. In *Tombs*, Ged goes to the Kargad lands, home of the savage blond barbarians who raid Gont in the earlier novel, to recover the lost half of the ring of Erreth-Akbe from the tombs. As long as the ring remains divided, Earthsea will know neither unity nor peace.

Ged goes seeking neither fame nor fortune. His goal is a

quest for knowledge. The two halves of the ring joined together form the "lost rune." To know the "true name" of a thing in Earthsea is to know its essence; so it is here. The true nature of unity is no longer understood because its sign is lost. This loss occurred long ago, when the attempts of the mage Erreth-Akbe to unify the world were defeated, and Earthsea slipped back into faction and darkness. This is no Christian fall which will end in a redemption. Ged follows Erreth as another man of wisdom and moral courage who attempts to bring harmony to a world. The tension between making and unmaking is constant and ongoing; man's continuing responsibility is to oppose the forces of disorder. The task is neverending, and utterly necessary. Against the permanence of chaos, mankind forms chains: the task passes from Estraven to Ai, from Erreth to Ged. In *Left Hand*, these forces of unmaking were collective bodies; in *Tombs*, their locus is an opposite sort — the tomb, the void. Yet significantly, this heart of darkness supports temples erected to a "god-king," maintained by a new political tyranny of "divine rights," and an oppressive priesthood.

The ring has been broken in two; one half was scattered to the winds, the other buried in the tombs. The world seems permanently in the grip of fear and greed. A false unity has been imposed on men by laws and priests. True harmony, in Le Guin, comes only from the gift freely given. The half of the ring in the world was thought buried at the ends of the earth — on a nameless sandbar along with the pair of royal siblings — and yet it returns. Ged is accidentally shipwrecked on the island in *Wizard*. Though rendered a near-savage from isolation, the woman nonetheless reaches out to mankind, and gives Ged the fragment. A chain of gifts begins which leads the hero to Selidor in the extreme west, where the dragon reveals to him the meaning of the object, then back to Atuan in the farthest east where, in the bowels of the tombs, the priestess Tenar gives him with the other half of the ring his greatest gift — his life.

At the heart of the public deed, we find a very private experience. The real drama is not Ged's, but Tenar's. She is faced with the same ordeal that Ged faced in *Wizard* — the coming of age. But she has no Ogion to guide her, and no school of wizardry to teach her. Her world is one that has sunk into ignorance and perversion. The proper balance of light and darkness, death and life, has been upset. Tenar is a person of great natural strength and imagination, but the priestesses guide her to darkness and denial of life. All feelings are repressed; her mind has nothing open to it but the dark labyrinth beneath the tombs. Ged's initiation began with water to life and a name. Tenar's name is taken from her in a grotesque ceremony in which the proper relationship between life and death is willfully inverted. A figure in white wields the sword of sacrifice, while one in black stays the hand at the last minute, and claims Tenar for the darkness. Thus, ironically, she becomes "the reborn" — her name is replaced by that of the "immortal" priestess Ahra. But this is eternal death, not life; the living are entombed, "eaten," swallowed by darkness: the dead become their master. In the case of the young child Tenar, it is Blake's "marriage hearse," the corruption of life at its source.

Ged is taken prisoner in the tombs. Tenar, the master of prisoners, holds him, and yet is fascinated by the presence of life in her dark domain. She will not yield him up to the God-King's priestess and death. Through their mutual contacts she comes, gradually, to see she is the one imprisoned, and not Ged. This mage shows her the marvels of the wide world beyond, but she claims superiority over him in the knowledge of her domain: "You know everything, wizard. But I know one thing — the one true thing!" Tenar is an intrepid explorer. She has gone farther than anyone else in the labyrinth, and now she pursues Ged with the same intellectual passion — she would know. It is only because her mind is great that she can make the breakthrough. Suddenly, she realizes Ged has gone farther than she even in her own realm of darkness. Seeing the scars on his face, she sees that "he knew death better than she did, even death." Their relationship is not only inverted, it changes levels as well. What was prisoner and jailer now becomes pupil and teacher. Ged knows one more thing — her name — and he gives it back to her. Only now, in accepting this gift, is she truly reborn. It is fruit from the tree of knowledge, for with her name the undying one must accept her mortality. The burden of life, she will discover, is a heavy one.

Once more, freedom comes only through acceptance of limitation. This is symbolized by the ring itself. Unlike the chains of the tombs, this "ring" is an armband which, in being joined and bound together, will free mankind. Tenar calls Ged a thief when she first meets him. But, just as the first half of the ring was freely given, this one must be too. It is Tenar who ultimately gives Ged both the ring and his freedom. In the tombs, literally, there is freedom only in joining. Tenar is surprised that Ged's magic seems powerless there. He must use it to keep from succumbing to darkness. But fighting the inner battle, he has not the strength to take the ring and return. Neither person alone, in fact, has the power to return to the light. Their only hope lies in the bond of mutual trust. The Ged who had lost faith in himself in *Wizard* was saved by a friend's kindness. Now Ged gives Tenar her name and life; in return, she gives him back water and life: "It was not the water alone that saved me. It was the strength of the hands that gave it." The union of these two is that of minds reaching out across the void. The result is a flood of light: from Ged's staff and hands a "white radiance" shows the walls of the great vault to be diamonds. Their opposite (the image runs through this novel and the next) is the spider, self-sufficient, weaving his futile web out of himself in dry, dark places.

Once again, darkness is emptiness, a negative thing with the power neither to make nor unmake. The tomb merely contains Ged and Tenar; it collapses of its own accord when they leave. Evil occurs only when men serve this darkness, and there are many degrees of evil in *Tombs*. When Tenar escapes into the world she feels a need to entomb herself again for the evil she has done. Ged tells her she was but "the vessel of evil" — it is now poured out: "You were never made for cruelty and darkness; you were made to hold light, as a lamp burning holds and gives its light. I found the lamp unlit . . ." More evil is the force that misuses this gift for life. But perversion is no absolute either; the priestess Kossil has corrupted herself. Her evilness can no longer be poured out, for she has taken the vessel within, and made of her mind a labyrinth. Her fear causes her to deny even the darkness, negating the order of things she has served all these years. The other servants of darkness have only wasted their lives: Thar's dignity, Manan's love, could find nothing to fulfill them. Kossil serves the destructive God-Kings, who have replaced the natural order with expediency and venality. Light is forbidden in the tomb, yet Kossil brings her feeble candle. She is no spider. The tomb collapses on her, digging by candlelight at empty graves, "like a great fat rat."

In a sense the last Earthsea novel, *Farthest Shore*, again plays out the struggle of *Wizard*, but this time on a different level, and in what appears a much more perilous and imperilled universe. Through the earlier novel there runs a deeper faith in the balance of things — it will right itself eventually, no matter what. Even if Ged had succumbed, and become an instrument of darkness, Vetch was still there to sink the boat. Ged had no intention of going to Iffish, his friend's home; a fortunate "chance" simply took him there. In FS, however, such checks and balances seem to have failed. A great wizard has yielded to the darkness, and his actions menace the equilibrium in Earthsea. To some extent, this wizard is again Ged's shadow, since Ged is largely responsible for the man's actions. Out of anger and vanity, Ged had once challenged a renegade mage named Cob, who had debased the summoning of the dead to a carnival trick, and dragged him to the wall that separates the land of the living from that of the dead. "Oh, a lesson you taught me, indeed," Cob later tells Ged, "but not the one you meant to teach! There I said to myself: 'I have seen death now, and I will not accept it.' "

Cob begins turning people from the natural rhythm of things by offering them eternal life. Against this irrational lure, knowledge is impotent — there must be power as well. The rune of peace has been procured, but the world remains divided. Without a central authority, a king on the throne, men and islands fall easy prey to him who would be Anti-King. The new leader will be young prince Arren, who comes to Roke and agrees to go with Ged to seek out the source of this evil.

Their journey takes them south, then west to land's end. At first, the object of their search is vague: it is a "break," a "breech." They seek a place, then a person, and eventually realize that what they are looking for is ultimately in themselves. Evil, in *Farthest Shore*, is more than ever "a web we men weave." The Anti-King is present in each man's mind, and their journey is that of each man to his death. But at the same time, it is also a journey through a series of real lands, people, and things; ultimately, it is a journey to Cob — an evildoer is destroyed, the breach in the universe is healed. The devastation is not only in their minds; real people are ravaged, leaders turn aside from duty, their lands fall to waste. More purposefully than ever, allegory functions here on several levels; the result is almost Dantesque. Symbolic levels are not only beautifully woven together, but firmly rooted in a concrete world which at every moment claims a reality of its own.

Ged soon realizes that he is not leading but following. Young Arren, although he accompanies the mage, is going his own way — to kingship, to the center of things. The path is, as usual, a circuitous and unexpected one. It takes him less to heroic deeds (his sword remains sheathed until the final adventure) than to out-of-the-way places: it is a true odyssey. To achieve their goal, both must cross the dry land of death. But this is a crossing Ged is ill-prepared for; the old man is at the end of his possibilities, and has already accepted death in the sunlight. Arren, however, is young; gradually he discovers his fear of death, and his desire for life. "It is your fear, your pain I follow," Ged tells him. But Arren in turn needs Ged and his wisdom of life. The task accomplished only through a bond of trust and love: "I use your love as a man burns a candle."

The physical journey may be read as a projection of Arren's fears, doubts and hopes. The trip south ends in a deadpoint — a slack sail and a paralyzed will. All along there is, significantly, little wind from Ged's magic. Arren in fact begins to doubt his power: what use is it? What can an old man and a boy do alone? *Farthest Shore* reflects Le Guin's interest in dreams. Arren dreams again and again — always visions of promise which end in chaos and darkness. The silk fields of Lorbanery become entangling spider webs. He hears the call to "come" during the seance with the drugged wizard Hare, and plunges deep into darkness. Later Roke itself falls victim to the same blight: students and masters begin to doubt their magic, recourse to crystal balls yield visions of unmaking, the Master Summoner loses himself in darkness. Arren becomes totally twisted around: he believes Ged is seeking death, and allies himself with the madman Sopli in the boat, whose madness is fear of death, water, and life itself. After the attack by the savages which wounds Ged, he himself is caught in the web of inaction; reality becomes a dream: "I could think of nothing, except that there was a way of not dying for me, if I could find it." Yet he cannot move, and life flows from him as from a broken scab.

The turning point is their rescue by the raft people, who beyond all land have built life and community over the abyss of the sea. Arren first believes this world a dream; but it is real, and the Long Dance is danced here as in all other lands of Earthsea; its people know joy and death. Here the young man learns that to refuse death is to refuse life — their relation is easy to see on the rafts, but is the same everywhere. More importantly, Ged shows him that no one is immune to this evil: "What is a good man . . . one who has no darkness in him? Look a little farther. Look into yourself! Did you not hear a voice say 'Come'? Did you not follow?" Arren is now freed to act; when the singers fail at the Long Dance, he can complete the song. But for him there is more to achieving selfhood than there was for young Ged. He is to be the king; the evil must be rooted out of the kingdom before he can rule. All nature comes to his aid, as helpful now as it was recalcitrant before. The dragon flies before them as their guide, and magewind fills the sails. The ancient powers join with men to combat the ultimate perversion. As with the tombs of Atuan, but on a vaster scale, the land of the dead is part of the balance. Cob has violated it.

The last pages of *Farthest Shore* are filled with a series of unforgetable images. Arren sees the dragons flying, and experiences a burst of joy in life, just as Estraven saw the fire mountains in the face of ruin, and thanked life for the gift. The "fierce willed concord" of the dragons' patterned flight. the beauty formed of a triad of "terrible strength, utter wildness and grace of reason," is the essence of life, to be gloried in. Orm Embar, the great dragon, dies impaled on the enemy's staff, like Mogien diving selflessly, and gives his life to save balance itself. Here, on the very spot where his ancestor Orm died fighting against man, he now dies fighting alongside him. More moving, however, is the confrontation with Cob at the heart of dryness. Under Ged's questions, his powers melt away, revealing the utter desolation of one who has traded the supreme gift, life, for nothing. He is withered, ugly, a spider of dust; he is blind when even the shades of the dead see, nameless when even they have names: when my body dies, Ged tells him, "I will be here, but only in name . . . in shadow . . . Do you not understand?" Death does not diminish life. It is *there*. "Here is nothing, dust and shadows." Cob is between, in limbo. And when he finally cries out for life, he sees that he has already forfeited it. Cob's tragedy, as with the Shing, is one of profound error; his "eternal life" is a colossal lie, and he is the first to be duped by it. This lie comes close to destroying mankind. It is not, however, an alien lure; it is man's deepest temptation.

Wisdom can heal the breach, but physical strength alone can make the return journey — Ged must rely on Arren to help him cross the Mountains of Pain and return to life. The young man, who failed Ged once before, now sets his will, and they escape back to the ocean shore, to water and life. To refuse death was to refuse life; in *Wizard*, here, the acceptance of death becomes a thirst for life. In his final voyage to the underworld, Arren, like the young Ged before him, learns what it is to be a man: "Only to man is given the gift of knowing he will die . . . Would you have the sea grow still and the tides cease to save one wave, yourself?"

The thrust of this epic is not simply "pre-Christian"; it is quite un-Christian, un-Western, in its naturalism, its reverence for the balance of life, and its refusal of transcendental values. The story is Arren's — his deed, like Ged's, is the acceptance of his own limits, his achievement of selfhood. He meets victory for the first time standing "alone, unpraised, at the end of the world." His victory is the act of closing his hand over a piece of dark stone from the Mountains of Pain. He thus accepts pain, and yet encapsulates it, enclosing it in warm life. Neither Ged nor Arren retreat from life in order to find it. Ged's "making" is the control of natural powers. More significantly, his successor is not a mage, but a king; the sword he wields may only be in the service of life, but it is nonetheless a sword. Power has become more and more necessary to the world of Earthsea. In this shift of focus from artist to ruler, Le Guin affirms the primacy of the social realm.

THE DISPOSSESSED

In a sense, Le Guin reaches her farthest shore in *Earthsea*. The geographic layout of this fantasy world is an exact parallel of her Hainish universe. In both, action has tended to take place, not at the center, but rather in the outlying reaches. At the end of *Tombs*, however, Tenar makes the journey inward, from the extreme east, to Havnor. And Arren, in *Farthest Shore*, returns from land's end to mount the throne at the center of things. Three of the four earlier Hainish novels are situated on worlds at the fringe of the known universe (even the Earth of *City* is no center but a wasteland). *Left Hand* is the far point, both in terms of time and space; thereafter, Le Guin begins to work backward. Both *Word* and "Vaster" still take place on distant planets, and their time is pre-*Rocannon*, before the discovery of mindspeech. *The Dispossessed* represents a retreat in spatial terms as well, from the periphery of the Hainish universe to its core. The twin planets are the Cetian worlds, oft mentioned, but never before seen. In linear time, TD represents the extreme point of retreat toward our present that Le Guin has yet explored. Terra has undergone eco-disaster, so we are definitely somewhere in the future. The event around which the novel revolves is the discovery of the theory of time which led to creation of the ansible, the faster-than-light communication device which first made the idea of a League possible. If Arren is the center of Earthsea, Shevek the physicist is the center of the Hainish planets.

And yet, *The Dispossessed*, though a return, goes farthest of all Le Guin's novels in investigating the problem of evil in a fundamentally monistic universe. In TD the author is writing explicit social commentary; it is, she states in a 1975 interview with Jonathan Ward, utopian fiction, and in a specific tradition — that of anarchist utopism from Thoreau to Paul Goodman, the "anti-centralized state." Obviously, Le Guin's Taoism and Goodman's Gestaltist concept of the "whole" form a common current. But in extending her world view into the realm of specific social speculation, Le Guin inherits certain problems as well. Goodman was troubled by the possibility of "un-natural" behavior: How can such a thing exist if nature is and always has been? Where could it have come from? Le Guin has, as we have seen, faced the same problem from the start in her Taoist universe. However tenacious and dangerous, evil has always been quantitative in nature — anti-natural actions, anti-kings. But is a qualitative evil possible; is there something in human nature itself which is unteachable, irremediable? Le Guin resists what Theodore Roszac calls the "satanic temptation." But in her strenuous, almost Puritanical probing of man's social conscience, she pushes her monist vision to new tensions and depths.

The problem in TD is not so much whether man can regulate himself; it is rather that he regulates himself naturally, and too much. The classic utopian question is asked here: What is the maximum personal freedom consistent with collective order? TD is less the story of social norms than that of the exceptional individual, Shevek. In any society, even the freest, his demands for freedom are excessive. Shevek's difficulties in realizing self are compounded; not only must he struggle against the self, but more fundamentally, against the walls men build around him. What Ged learned was the responsibility of the individual to the whole. In this new novel, there is another aspect: society has a responsibility to the creative man as well. He is its future; and if he is prevented from growing, will it not perish? Ged led Arren to kingship. The bases of authority are much simpler in Earthsea: the young "rowan tree" has deep roots both in the natural and racial past of his world. But where are the roots of men in TD?

On Urras they have their property; the "dispossessed" of Anarres have not even that. This anarchist society offers no institutional base but that of the principle of continuous revolution. Le Guin takes things to their roots in human nature itself. But instead of freedom, we find strictures, created from within. Cob feared death; people in TD fear life itself, bold vision, the promise of the future. There are no unmakers to combat; each man unmakes himself, and together they unmake society. This intractability is as close as Le Guin has come to the "unnatural" — corruption at the human heart of things, blight at the source of power itself. The breach Shevek sets out to heal is the hardest one yet faced: that between the intransigent multitude and the man of vision.

Le Guin has called TD an "ambiguous utopia." The physical setting alone, as compared to that of *Left Hand*, reveals the complexity of the problem. We find little easy balance or fortunate paradox here. In LHD, there were two societies; surrounding both were the planet, a common nature, and a common culture in which men could seek their roots. Social reality may not be solid, but the base is. TD has two separate worlds, two distinct natures, two radically different societies. The only thing they have in common is that both are inhabited by men. Furthermore, Le Guin gives a twist to the simplistic utopian dream of the perfect society in a perfect setting. Urras, the world with the capitalist society, is lush, green, and bountiful. Anarres, the anarchist planet, is harsh, moonlike, and barren.

Urras is not planet Earth, but it is close enough to be its double. It has more water than land (Anarres is a "dry" world, with huge land masses and few seas). There is a familiar power balance between a capitalist state and a totalitarian "socialist" one; behind the mask of opposing ideologies is the common urge for power, possession, and dominance. There is even an underdeveloped "third world" nation, Benbili, the scene of constant political meddling and military interventions on the part of both superpowers. And finally, there is the same variety and abundance of nature one finds on Earth (on Anarres, man is isolated, and there are fish but no land mammals). Ironically, part of the historical background to the

Hainish books is the presence of a Terra which long ago destroyed its own natural world. The Urrasti have learned to conserve, and the planet is in no danger of eco-disaster, or apparently of any other disaster. There is a stable cold war balance, a pax urrastiana; a little blood is shed now and then to serve as a permanent stimulus to the competitive spirit, but basically things are quiet. The Urrasti are preparing to move into space, but for that they need Shevek's theory.

The only danger, it appears, is from Anarres, which has little physical force, but a large and dangerous idea. When Shevek leaps the gap between planets, he comes as the incarnation of the anarchist ideal. But why is it so explosive? The Terran Ambassador wonders too: "The government here is not despotic. The rich are very rich indeed, but the poor are not so very poor. They are neither enslaved nor starving. Why aren't they satisfied with bread and speeches?" Shevek's ideal strikes at the core of a society which has developed a privileged class of owners and managers, and relegated all others to a life of drudgery. The men in revolt demand the freedom to realize their individual lives to the extent their talents and inclinations may allow. And yet, even the caste system is not that rigid — there are no hereditary guilds or other dystopian nightmares. The entrepreneurial spirit is, in fact, still alive. Oiie's grand-father scrubbed floors; his father was a self-made man. Nor is the revolt the product of any middle-class change of "consciousness." Their sons are surprisingly docile university students — they want the competitive distinctions, just what it takes to get ahead. Those few who rebel are a genuine proletariat, demanding less that the wealth be shared than that their lives have value.

Estraven was exiled; Shevek and his people are "dispossessed." The depth of their refusal of property is measured by the fact that they chose to settle a place where there is little or nothing to possess. Estraven at least knew that home was "the hills of Estre;" he could hold fast to the thing. But if Anarres is the place without things, where is Shevek's home? The only thing these people have is each other, a society, a social ideal. Yet, both as men and as Odonians, they are not as completely cut off from Urras as they might like to believe.

The central park in the Anarresti capital is a carefully tended grove of trees from Urras. And Odo, the founder of their society, never saw this world nor even conceived of it; she wrote her manifestos in prison on Urras, and lies buried there. When Shevek leaves for Urras then, he is both leaving home and going home. Only by making that jump does he begin to discover the complexity of time and human existence.

The two social systems in TD are, in the eyes of their proponents, incompatible. But at their roots, how different are they? A comparison with *Left Hand* is instructive. Orgoreyn is centralized, controlled in a way that goes against human nature; the natural society is the anarchistic one which flourishes in Karhide — collective farms that are truly voluntary, communal villages, hospitality, mutual aid. Totalitarianism is clearly a misunderstanding of man's nature, now made law and enforced by police. If man is given the freedom to choose, he will make a society which respects freedom.

In TD, Le Guin goes deeper. There is no totalitarian society. Both of these societies, the capitalist one in A-Io as well as the anarchist one on Anarres, make a direct appeal to human nature. Both are founded on a demand for freedom — freedom to acquire and possess, freedom to fulfill oneself in work and life. And both reveal a rapid demand, from within, that this freedom be regulated. Rampant capitalism of the *laissez faire* sort is no longer tolerated in A-Io. In this well-regulated state, the madmen and robber barons are museum pieces. Vea tells Shevek that "things like that couldn't happen now." On the other hand, regulation is not brutal or mindless — there is latitude. A-Io has no mind police; the press is "free," a harmless outlet for otherwise dangerous frustrations. More significant however is that men on Anarres as well seem unable to tolerate excess of freedom, in spite of their code of permanent rebellion. The "madmen" they seek to contain, by conventions if not by laws, are ironically the true anarchists themselves.

The wall building of the Urrasti is easier to see because it is linked to possession of property — goods and humans. Vea's credo is simple: "I don't care about other people, and nobody else does either. They pretend to. I don't want to pretend. I want to be free!" But her idea of being free is survival of the fittest. Women in this society strive to "run the men," but paradoxically, can do so only at the expense of any real freedom; to rule, they must become the possessions of these men. Shevek sees the Urrasti in the same light that Thoreau saw the men of Concord — they are slaves to their possessions: "You the possessors are possessed. You are all in jail. Each alone, solitary, with a heap of what he owns." In contrast, Shevek stands out as a "natural man" on Urras — spontaneous, direct, heedless of taboos and sexual barriers. Shevek however is not one who, like Thoreau, has practiced the doctrine of "simplicity" entirely of his own volition. In great part, he and all Annaresti have been forced to do without by the harshness of their world. This "natural" behavior is in reality a product of trial and error, of learning what is essential. In darker moments, the Anarresti themselves come to see anarchism and solidarity as things born only of adversity. Shevek meets and overcomes this doubt both on Urras and on Anarres, where, during the drought, he realizes that adversity brings forth brutal instincts to survive, and impersonal bureaucratic disregard for individual life.

Shevek discovers more formidable walls in his own society — those men build within. In spite of the basic Odonian tenet that the duty of the individual is to accept no rule, he finds the Anarresti let themselves too easily be ruled: "We fear our neighbor's opinion more than we respect our own freedom of choice . . . just try stepping over the line, just in imagination, and see how you feel . . . We've made laws, laws of conventional behavior, built walls around ourselves, and we can't see them, because they're part of our thinking." Shevek was earlier told by Bedap that the will to dominate is as central in human beings as the impulse to mutual aid. Through his dealings with Sabul, the empire-building "superior" who preempts his theories, he comes to believe it. But he cannot let his wife take the blame for his giving in — the fault is his. Each man has his own "internalized Sabul — convention, moralism, fear of social ostracism, fear of being different, fear of being free!" Natural man is not as natural as he seems; he too has a superego. Social conscience is as stern a regulator here as on Urras; only the way of aggressing is different. The Urrasti violate by breaking into a man's castle. The Anarresti transgress, and step across the invisible lines of society, as Shevek did at the beginning of the novel, as he has been doing all his life. This is the way of anarchy; the Odonians took the first step; will they now forgive this exceptional man for taking the second — the "metaphysical risk"?

The two worlds are so different and yet so alike, so close and yet so far apart. They can never be linked, put into any adequate temporal relationship one to the other, until Shevek makes his journey. His situation is analagous to that of Falk in *City* — the only point of contact between two worlds is the hero's mind, the act of will and understanding that will join them. Shevek's situation is much more complex. From the start, he has memory; he goes to break down walls, to bind the two worlds together. This naivete comes from his ignorance of the relationship of Urras and Anarres in time, and of the nature of time itself. In one sense, Urras is Anarres' past, a thing abandoned. But as the mining ships from Urras show, this cleavage is a figment of the Anarresti mind. To those on Urras, the twin planet is very much part of their material present — a mining colony. To Shevek the frustrated physicist, however, Urras has become the future, the place where he will complete his work. The result of his going is the discovery that Urras really is Anarres' past. But in order to see this, he must first break free of new walls and a new dilemma: "He had come to love Urras, but what good was his yearning love. He was not part of it. Nor was he part of the world of his birth." At this point, to love both is to lose both past and future, to be doubly alienated. Later, he will realize that only in choosing both can he regain a past and a future. Only thus can he move toward a future which is also a return. The solution to this dilemma is the creation of his Unified Theory of Time.

This theory is more than just another elaborate metaphor for the old idea of change in permanence. It is, quite literally, the result of one man's struggle, step by step, to learn how he is the child of time. Shevek knows both worlds successively — like the arrow shot at the tree, they should never meet. But through memory and dream, he comes to know them simultaneously as well. But if succession is really a subjective phenomenon, not an objective one, how can man be an actor at all in any causal sense in time? Worse, how can he be responsible if what he does has already been done? Sequency and freedom of action are not resolved in simultanist mysticism, the arrow replaced by the circle of time. Again, there are two options in what seems a dilemma — not to choose, or to choose both. It is Shevek's ultimate acceptance of both worlds, rather than a choice between them or a denial of both, which permits him to see the pattern, to complete his theory, and opt for Anarres. He could not have finished his work without this voyage to Urras. For there he discovers another past — "Ainsetain's" attempt at a unifying field theory. In the light of the Terran's limitations, his walls, Shevek sees that his own search for certainty has itself been a prison: "In the region of the unprovable, or even the disprovable, lay the only chance for breaking out of the circle and going ahead." His moment of truth is no mystical vision; it is a return to concrete reality, a tangible world neither Urras nor Anarres: "he was glad to be back among these familiar objects, back in his own world — for at this instant the difference between this planet and that one . . . was no more significant to him than the difference between two grains of sand . . . There was no more exile. He had seen the foundations of the universe, and they were solid."

Odo's thought is one of analogies; there are no compart-ments, only correspondances. The binding factor between levels of reality is always man. He is, as Shevek proves in life and theory, the dynamic element in the universal balance. The same is true, he discovers, in terms of state and individual: "That the Odonian society on Anarres had fallen short of the ideal did not . . . lessen his responsibility to it . . . Sacrifice might be demanded of the individual, but never compromise: for though only the society could give security and stability, only the individual had the power of moral choice — the power of change, the essential function of life." Shevek's theory, a choice for uncertainty, is a moral option for the future. "By simply assuming the validity of real coexistence he was left free to use the lovely geometries of relativity." On the political level he can now choose the relative freedom of Anarres. He sees Sabul's possessiveness in a new light: what was psychopathy on Anarres is rational behavior on Urras.

More dangerous than the imperfections of Anarresti society is the Edenic temptation Keng the Terran offers Shevek. To her people, who have destroyed their world, Urras is paradise lost. Held by the bleakness of their past, they can neither join with the present (they are "outside" it, they "envy" it), nor conceive of hope for the future. Keng, like Shevek before, is between two worlds powerless to be born. But now Shevek's hard-won knowledge offers hope and a future, this time on a cosmic scale. Through the ansible Keng can rejoin her past. Shevek standing before her unites past and present in the promise of a future: "You are like somebody from our own past, the old idealists . . . and yet I don't understand you, as if you were trying to tell me of future things; and yet, as you say, you are here, now!" To Shevek, there is but one choice, one direction: we cannot come to you, you must come to us. Ketho the Hainishman is the one who makes that choice. His, the oldest race, is also bound by its past to some terrible "guilt." But out of their long experience they have made a perpetual balanced present, a world of the golden mean. What they lack, however, is a dynamic sense of the future; they are born mature, and cannot laugh. What Shevek's vision of time gives them is this lost youth. Keng said: "*we* forfeited our right to Anarres long ago." But Ketho sees that, although his race may know anarchism, he the individual does not. He has been there, yet not been there.

In the complex structure of TD, Shevek's theory of time is the principle which shapes the narrative whole. There are two alternating strands: the scenes on Urras, the narrative present, and those on Anarres which recount Shevek's past, the events leading to his departure. The end seems to turn back to the beginning, as in a circle. The first two chapters tell of twin births: Shevek leaves Anarres for a new life on Urras, Shevek is born on Anarres. This latter birth begins a gradual falling away from his society, and leads inexorably to his departure. The voyage to Urras, on the other hand, instead of bringing a new life, turns Shevek gradually back toward Anarres. From an initial point of deepest alienation he begins working his way back, until he finally decides to return. These are two different worlds, and a man moving in two different directions. And yet each pair of chapters, from one to twelve, mirror each other. An example is chapters five and six. On Urras Shevek meets people — Chifoilisk the Thuvian, Atro the aristocrat, Oiie the bitter unsatisfied man whose private world is his sanctuary — and the scales fall from his eyes. In all of this, the only being he can call "brother" is a pet otter. On Anarres he meets Bedap and his circle — scales again fall from his eyes. Then he meets Takver, who becomes his lifelong partner; a more fulfilling relationship is established, the balance falls in favor of Anarres. The chapter on Anarres ends with Shevek in Takver's arms; on Urras it ends with him dreaming of her. In both he gazes at a moon, dreams of a moon that is cold, a vision of death. The two chapters interlock here — going away is coming home — but the overriding factor is Takver and her love. *The Dispossessed* has thirteen chapters, however. The going away at the end of chapter twelve has perhaps coincided with the coming home — there is balance. But there is also asymmetry — the emphasis is on change.

Le Guin's ambiguous utopia seems to end on an optimistic note. Shevek laughs for joy as the ship heads down for Anarres: "I will sleep with Takver tonight." We remember however Estraven and Ai skiing off laughing into the ice of death. Perhaps Shevek too will come through this time. But in opening walls, he is bound to encounter new ones and stronger ones. The stormy discord of his leaving, with mother against son, is now the threat of mob violence. The society that has misapplied Odo can easily misconstrue Shevek, or kill him. What hope is there for the creative man, the visionary, faced with this unregenerate human nature? A Le Guin story of the same year, "The Stars Below," is more pessimistic in its implications. Here a Galileo-like hero has his instruments smashed by the authorities and is driven underground into a mine. Befriended by the miners, he works with them until, seized once again by intellectual curiosity, he breaks from the community and pursues the "stars below" to his destruction. The miners who could not understand him later go to the spot he indicated, and strike silver, and a vein of crystals. There are all kinds of men in this tale: brutal fanatics, the Count who saves him out of simple friendship, the kindly but uncomprehending miners, and the visionary hero himself. But what is the meaning here? Certainly there is light to be found in this darkness as well as in the sky. But the man of imagination is forced by mankind, not just society, into an inverted world below. However noble the goal, the end is futile.

CONCLUSION

Where will Le Guin go from here? One can only speculate. A likely direction is inward, away from the collective drama, toward the individual which lies at its roots. The award-winning story "The Day Before the Revolution," written as a sequel to *The Dispossessed*, is perhaps symptomatic. Le Guin again goes back in time to relate the story of Odo, founder of the anarchist movement. Interestingly, the piece does not deal with her birth nor the revolutionary years, nor even with the writing of the *Principles* during her creative period. It recounts her death.

Except for its setting, DBR is hardly science fiction at all. It is simply an account of the last day in the life of a sick old woman. She tries to walk to the park, is unable, turns back to die in her room on the eve of the revolution she had brought about. The landscape is familiar — city streets and slums. The people are average, unidealized, and unheroic. The theme is the eternal one of old age and death. In *The Dispossessed* Shevek has both a past and a present; his actions bring about a new future. So have Odo's, but those actions are all past; her present is physical decay. In the movement she founded she is no longer a vital force, but rather a monument.

The focus in this story is harshly realistic. Le Guin reaches behind the facade of ideals to reveal the basic drives that move humanity. Odo acknowledges sex and vanity; she acknowledges the private happiness sacrificed and lost. As a true anarchist, she refuses the static situation, and questions everything. In her old age, however, this has simply become testiness. Odo discovers the true limits of change — death. But there is no heroic rushing into it this time; her body just fails, and she is forced to accept. For Ai in *Left Hand*, restoration of the general balance could not compensate for Estraven's death. And in TD the private tragedy of Bedap, who gave his life to an ideal and found himself alone, seems equally inexplicable. There are different kinds of deaths. Odo experiences both. At the moment of her greatest public success, the day before her revolution, she sees her life as a series of failures. And her spirit, that part of her still vitally alive, is defeated by the flesh. In this story as in the companion novel, there is a circle — a going out coincides with a coming home. But what balances the "general strike" is now the "private stroke." She meets her fate not laughing, but with wry irony.

The short story remains a short story, the perfect instrument for probing in depth within a larger framework. It tells nothing as to the nature of Le Guin's next large frame. But it does represent a far point. In the dynamic of change in permanence, the balance has come down hard on the side of human mutability.

But other directions are possible for Le Guin, as her latest story, "The New Atlantis," shows. We again move backward, to a Terra in the throes of ecological disaster. The world here is a collective one, but in it the great men have no chance to bring change. They are a huddled group of broken men, dreamers who build a solar cell while their world sinks. Balance is present: as we go down, the old sunken continent Atlantis rises and is created anew. The ugliness of our adspeak is juxtaposed with poetry of creation. Yet ambiguities remain: if there is rapport between our great spirits and the voices of Atlantis, to what end is communication? It is an either/or situation; they emerge, but we are gone: "We are here. Where have you gone?" Worse, is this Atlantis but the dream, the hallucination, of a dying race? Mankind does not, as before, return from the verge of destruction; he is replaced by a myth. Balance remains, but man has lost his central position at its heart. In this story, at least, he no longer seems a vital force. Has ambiguity given way to pessimism? In these two stories, the individual life ends in death, the collective existence in annihilation.

BIOGRAPHY & BIBLIOGRAPHY

URSULA KROEBER LE GUIN was born October 21, 1929, at Berkeley, California, the daughter of Dr. Alfred L. Kroeber, a noted anthropologist, and Theodora (Kracaw) Le Guin, a writer. She graduated from Radcliffe College in 1951, and later obtained an M.A. from Columbia University in French Renaissance Studies (1952). Her first professional sale, "April in Paris," appeared in *Fantastic Stories* in September, 1962; her first book was published by Ace Books four years later. Le Guin has twice won double Hugo/Nebula Awards for Best Science Fiction Novel of the year, for *The Left Hand of Darkness* and *The Dispossessed*. In addition, she has also received a National Book Award for *The Farthest Shore*, a Newbery Silver Medal for *The Tombs of Atuan*, a Nebula for "The Day Before the Revolution," Jupiter Awards for *The Dispossessed* and "The Day Before the Revolution," and Hugo Awards for "The Word for World Is Forest" and "The Ones Who Walk Away from Omelas." She lives with her husband and three children in Portland, Oregon.

A list of her published books follows:

1. *Rocannon's World.* Ace Double, New York, 1966, 117p, Paper, Novel
2. *Planet of Exile.* Ace Double, New York, 1966, 113p, Paper, Novel
3. *City of Illusions.* Ace, New York, 1967, 160p, Paper, Novel
4. *A Wizard of Earthsea.* Parnassus Press, Berkeley, 1968, 205p, Cloth, Novel
5. *The Left Hand of Darkness.* Ace, New York, 1969, 286p, Paper, Novel (note: this edition is the true first; the hardcover from Walker appeared later)
6. *The Tombs of Atuan.* Atheneum, New York, 1971, 163p, Cloth, Novel
7. *The Lathe of Heaven.* Charles Scribner's Sons, New York, 1971, 184p, Cloth, Novel

8. *The Farthest Shore.* Atheneum, New York, 1972, 223p, Cloth, Novel

9. *From Elfland to Poughkeepsie.* Pendragon Press, Portland, 1973, 33p, Paper, Nonfiction

10. *The Dispossessed.* Harper & Row, New York, 1974, 341p, Cloth, Novel

11. *Wild Angels.* Capra Press, Santa Barbara, 1975, 50p, Paper, Verse Coll.

12. *The Wind's Twelve Quarters.* Harper & Row, New York, 1975, 303p, Cloth, Coll.

13. *Dreams Must Explain Themselves.* Algol Press, New York, 1975, 37p, Paper, Coll. (includes a short story, essay, and an interview)

14. *The Word for World Is Forest.* Berkley, New York, 1976, 189p, Cloth, Novel (This story originally appeared in *Again, Dangerous Visions,* an anthology edited by Harlan Ellison for Doubleday in 1972)

The chronology of the Hainish Cycle runs roughly in this order: *The Dispossessed,* "Vaster Than Empires and More Slow," "The Word for World Is Forest," *Rocannon's World, Planet of Exile, City of Illusions, The Left Hand of Darkness.*

A number of short scholarly articles have been published about Le Guin's work in a wide variety of sources; the best of these were commissioned for a special Le Guin issue of *Science-Fiction Studies* (No. 7, November 1975).

now available in the Borgo Press series:

Robert A. Heinlein: Stranger in His Own Land,
    by George Edgar Slusser B-201

The Beach Boys: Southern California Pastoral,
    by Bruce Golden B-202

Alistair MacLean: The Key Is Fear,
    by Robert A. Lee B-203

The Attempted Assassination of John F. Kennedy,
    by Lucas Webb B-204

The Farthest Shores of Ursula K. Le Guin,
    by George Edgar Slusser B-205

forthcoming titles (April 1977):

Up Your Asteroid! A Science Fiction Farce,
    by C. Everett Cooper B-206

The Bradbury Chronicles,
    by George Edgar Slusser B-207

John D. MacDonald and the Colorful World
of Travis McGee,
    by Frank D. Campbell, Jr. B-208

Harlan Ellison: Unrepentant Harlequin,
    by George Edgar Slusser B-209

just $1.95 at your favorite bookstore

The Borgo Press
P.O. Box 2845
San Bernardino, CA 92406